First World War
and Army of Occupation
War Diary
France, Belgium and Germany

31 DIVISION
Divisional Troops
Royal Army Veterinary Corps
41 Mobile Veterinary Section
15 March 1916 - 30 April 1919

WO95/2355/2

The Naval & Military Press Ltd
www.nmarchive.com
Published in association with The National Archives

Published by

The Naval & Military Press Ltd

Unit 10 Ridgewood Industrial Park,
Uckfield, East Sussex,
TN22 5QE England
Tel: +44 (0) 1825 749494

www.naval-military-press.com

www.nmarchive.com

This diary has been reprinted in facsimile from the original. Any imperfections are inevitably reproduced and the quality may fall short of modern type and cartographic standards.

© Crown Copyright
Images reproduced by permission of The National Archives, London, England, 2015.

Contents

Document type	Place/Title	Date From	Date To
Heading	WO95/2355/2 41 Mobile Veterinary Section		
Heading	31st Division Divl Troops 41st Mobile Vety Secn 1916 Mar-Apr 1919		
War Diary	Longpre	15/03/1916	29/03/1916
War Diary	Louvencourt	30/03/1916	21/05/1916
Heading	41 M Vet Sec Vol 4 XXXI		
War Diary	Field.	22/05/1916	08/07/1916
Miscellaneous	D.A.G. 3rd Echelon	22/05/1916	22/05/1916
Heading	War Diary Of 41th Mob. Vet. Section 1st July To 31st July 1916 Vol 5		
War Diary	Field.	09/07/1916	31/08/1916
Heading	War Diary. Mobile Veterinary Section 31st Division September 1916 Vol 7		
War Diary	Field.	01/09/1916	30/09/1916
Heading	War Diary 41st Mobile Veterinary Section 31st Division October 1916 Volume 8		
War Diary	Field	01/10/1916	24/10/1916
War Diary	Authie	25/10/1916	31/10/1916
Heading	War Diary. 41st Mobile Veterinary Section November 1916 Volume XI Vol 9		
War Diary	Authie	01/11/1916	14/11/1916
War Diary	Field.	15/11/1916	30/11/1916
Heading	War Diary 41st Mobile Veterinary Section December 1916 Vol 10		
War Diary	Field	01/12/1916	31/12/1916
Heading	War Diary 41st Mobile Veterinary Section 31st Division January 1917 Vol XI		
War Diary	Field	01/01/1917	31/01/1917
Heading	War Diary. 41st Mobile Veterinary Section 31st Division February 1917. Volume XIV. Vol 12		
War Diary	Field	01/02/1917	28/02/1917
Heading	War Diary. 41. Mobile Veterinary Section 31st Division March 1917. Volume XV Vol 13		
War Diary	In The Field.	01/03/1917	11/03/1917
War Diary	Field.	12/03/1917	31/03/1917
Heading	War Diary. 41st Mobile Veterinary Section 31st Division April 1917. Volume XVI Vol 14		
War Diary	In The Field.	01/04/1917	30/04/1917
Heading	War Diary. 41st Mobile Vet Section 31st Division May 1917. Volume XVII Vol.15		
War Diary	In The Field	01/05/1917	31/05/1917
Heading	War Diary. 41st Mobile Veterinary Section 31st Division June 1917 Volume XVIII Vol 16		
War Diary	Field	01/06/1917	30/06/1917
Heading	War Diary. 41st Mobile Veterinary Section 31st Division July 1917 Volume XIX Vol 17		
War Diary	Field	01/07/1917	23/07/1917
War Diary	In The Field.	24/07/1917	31/07/1917
Heading	War Diary. 41st Mobile Veterinary Section 31st Division August 1917 Volume XX Vol 18		

War Diary	Field	01/08/1917	11/08/1917
War Diary	In The Field.	12/08/1917	31/08/1917
Heading	War Diary. 41st Mobile Vet Section 31st Division September 1917. Volume XXI Vol 19		
War Diary	In The Field.	01/09/1917	12/09/1917
War Diary	Field.	13/09/1917	30/09/1917
Heading	War Diary. 41st Mobile Vet Section 31st Division October 1917. Volume XXII Vol 20		
War Diary	Field.	01/10/1917	31/10/1917
Heading	War Diary. 41st Mobile Veterinary Section 31st Division November 1917. Volume XXIII Vol 21		
War Diary	Field	01/11/1917	31/03/1918
Heading	Ambulance Horse Horse. Front		
War Diary	Field.	01/04/1918	30/04/1918
Heading	War Diary. 41st Mob. Vet. Section May 1918 Volume XXIX Vol 27		
War Diary	Field.	01/05/1918	31/07/1918
War Diary	In The Field.	01/08/1918	31/08/1918
War Diary	Field.	01/09/1918	28/02/1919
War Diary	Blendecques	01/03/1919	23/04/1919
War Diary	Longuenesse	24/04/1919	30/04/1919

WO95/2355/2

41 Mobile Veterinary Section

31ST DIVISION
DIVL TROOPS

41ST MOBILE VETY SECN
1916 MAR — 1915 - APR 1919

Army Form C. 2118.

WAR DIARY
or
INTELLIGENCE SUMMARY.
(Erase heading not required.)

Instructions regarding War Diaries and Intelligence Summaries are contained in F. S. Regs., Part II. and the Staff Manual respectively. Title pages will be prepared in manuscript.

Place	Date	Hour	Summary of Events and Information	Remarks and references to Appendices
LONGPRÉ	15/10		Daily routine	PwB
"	16/10		Section opened for reception of sick animals	PwB
"	17/10		Sent to WIRY-au-MONT and collected sick horse from an inhabitant	PwB
"	18/10		" LA CHAUSSÉE for sick horse but found it had been collected	PwB
"	19/10		Daily routine. One case of Glanders in 170 Bde RFA	PwB
"	20/10		Went to ABBEVILLE met ADVS for demonstration in Mallein test	PwB
"	21/10		Daily routine. Gassed out and dried improved accordn.	PwB
"	22/10		Visited units in LONGPRÉ.	PwB
"	23/10		Visited units at FLIXECOURT.	PwB
"	24/10		Daily routine	PwB
"	25/10		Railed 18 horses and 3 mules to ABBEVILLE	PwB
"	26/10		Visited units at FLIXECOURT	PwB
"	27/10		Took one G/te GS limbered wagon to ABBEVILLE and exchanged it for	PwB
"	28/10		a float. Railed 12 horses and 3 mules to ABBEVILLE	PwB
"			Marched from LONGPRÉ to VIGNACOURT under OC 12 MoYeL	PwB

WAR DIARY or INTELLIGENCE SUMMARY.

Army Form C. 2118.

(Erase heading not required.)

Place	Date	Hour	Summary of Events and Information	Remarks and references to Appendices
	29/6		Marched from VIGNACOURT to BEAUVAL. Had difficulty in getting the float (horse ambulance) which was later with section over our high road.	Pub
LOUVENCOURT	30/6		Marched from BEAUVAL to LOUVENCOURT. Billeted at LOUVENCOURT	Pub
"	31/6		The float is not suitable when on the move. Opened the Section for the reception of sick animals in the grounds of Chateau at LOUVENCOURT. Saddlery received from Ordnance	Pub
"	1/7		Assisted with malleining of 165 Brigade by mtd Armee preferred method.	Pub
"	2/7		Visited malleined horses of 165 Brigade RFA and applied the hypodermic test but inspecious reactions Received the stolen horses from ASSEVILLERS	Pub
"	3/7		with ARUS again visited malleined horses of 165 Bde RFA	Pub
"	4/7		Stayed out.	Pub
"	5/7		Malleined mules of 221 Coy ASC Raised 2 H, 3 M to 22 Vety Hospital	Pub
"	6/7		" 222 " " and visited reactors in 221 Coy	Pub
"	7/7		Inspected mules of 222 Coy ASC	Pub

41 MUSe
Army Form C. 2118.
Vol 2

WAR DIARY
or
INTELLIGENCE SUMMARY.
(Erase heading not required.)

Instructions regarding War Diaries and Intelligence Summaries are contained in F.S. Regs., Part II. and the Staff Manual respectively. Title pages will be prepared in manuscript.

Place	Date	Hour	Summary of Events and Information	Remarks and references to Appendices
LOUVENCOURT	8/16		Injected mules of 223 Coy A.S.C. Four horses died of incective poisoning	Ruds
"	9/16		Inspected mules of 223 Coy and mallened the animals of 224 Coy 28 Lds	Ruds
"	10/16		Railed 14 horses and 1 mule to ABBEVILLE	Ruds
"	11/16		Nove S & S Bethupt a rooster to mallein test + nede M. d Cows	Ruds
"			not- glandered	
"	12/16		Routine work	Ruds
"	13/16		Rifle inspection	Ruds
"	14/16		Railed 6 horses and 2 mules to ABBEVILLE	Ruds
"	15/16		Went to DOULLENS and thought order for the horse standings	Ruds
"	16/16		Sunday	Ruds
"	17/16		Routine work	Devs?
"	18/16		Mullined 125 mules of 21st S.A.C. — Railed 14 horses v 2 mules	Ruds
"	19/16		" " " to ABBEVILLE	Ruds
"	20/16		Inspected 16 horses to ABBEVILLE	Ruds
"	21/16		Section inspected by et Col V.O. 4th Army	Ruds
"	22/16		Railed 17 horses to ABBEVILLE	Ruds

Army Form C. 2118.

WAR DIARY
or
INTELLIGENCE SUMMARY.
(Erase heading not required.)

Place	Date	Hour	Summary of Events and Information	Remarks and references to Appendices
LOUVENCOURT	23/4		Easter Sunday. Railed 8 horses to ABBEVILLE.	RuB
"	24/4		Medical inspn of 31st Div: Ammn: Col. Railed 14 horses and 1 mule to ABBEVILLE.	RuB
"	25/4		Inspected mules of 31st S.A.C. Railed two sick food mules to ABBEVILLE	RuB
"	26/4		Inspected mules of the 31st S.A.C.	RuB
"	27/4		16 horses railed to No 23 Vety Hospital at ABBEVILLE	RuB
"	28/4		Routine work	RuB
"	29/4		Routine work.	RuB
"	30/4		Made Post Mortem on Mule at THIEVRES. Discovered rupture of the spleen, the spleen measuring 30" x 12" & the base of the lungs. The rupture was 6".	RuB
"	"		Rifle Inspection.	RuB
"	1/5		Railed 16 horses and 2 mules to ABBEVILLE.	RuB
"	2/5		Routine work. Returned with Brigher Mallein 5" notables Inspector went to DOULLENS and got a lorry load of oats.	RuB
"	3/5			RuB
"	4/5		Railed 17 horses and two mules to ABBEVILLE.	RuB
"	5/5		Completed mallein testing of 2 Cav & 4th Army Aux Horse Coy	RuB

Army Form C. 2118.

WAR DIARY
or
INTELLIGENCE SUMMARY.
(Erase heading not required.)

Instructions regarding War Diaries and Intelligence Summaries are contained in F.S. Regs., Part II. and the Staff Manual respectively. Title pages will be prepared in manuscript.

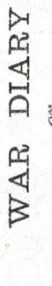

Place	Date	Hour	Summary of Events and Information	Remarks and references to Appendices
LOUVENCOURT	6/6		Daily Routine	App 1
"	7/6		Railed 19 horses to ABBEVILLE.	App 2
"	8/6		Daily Routine	App 3
"	9/6		Daily Routine	App 4
"	10/6		Daily routine	
"	11/6		Took over Vety. charge of the 12th Infy Bde	App 5
"	12/6		Routine work	App 6
"	13/6		Sixty horses and three mules railed to ABBEVILLE	App 7
"	14/6		Routine work.	App 8
"	15/6		Routine work. Inspection the horses of the 12th Infy. Bde.	App 9
"	16/6		Routine work	App 10
"	17/6		Railed 9 horses and 1 mule to ABBEVILLE	App 11
"	18/6		Routine work.	App 12
"	19/6		Routine work	App 13
"	20/6		Railed 9 horses and 1 foal to ABBEVILLE	App 14
"	21/6		Routine work	App 15

41 Am Vet Soc
Vol 4

(XXX)

41 M VerSie

Army Form C. 2118.

Vol 4

WAR DIARY
or
INTELLIGENCE SUMMARY.
(Erase heading not required.)

Instructions regarding War Diaries and Intelligence Summaries are contained in F.S. Regs., Part II. and the Staff Manual respectively. Title pages will be prepared in manuscript.

Place	Date	Hour	Summary of Events and Information	Remarks and references to Appendices
Field	22/5		Moved Section to THIEVRES and established a collecting post at Poilked Purs	AppB
"	23/5		Railed 30 horses to ASSEVILLE	AppB
"	24/5		Capt Bamford ASC proceeds on leave Major Matthews AVC takes over charge	AppM
"	25/5		Routine work	AppM
"	26/5		Routine work	AppM
"	27/5		Routine work	AppM
"	28/5		Routine work	AppM
"	29/5		Routine work	AppM
"	30/5		Routine work	AppM
"	31/5		Routine work	AppM
"	1/6		Routine work	AppM
"	2/6		Routine work	AppM
"	3/6		Capt Bamford resumed duty	AppM
"	4/6		Routine work	AppB
"	5/6		Took over NetR charge of 31st SAC. Routine work	AppB
"	6/6		Railed 11 horses and 4 mules to ASSEVILLE	AppB

Army Form C. 2118.

WAR DIARY
or
INTELLIGENCE SUMMARY.
(Erase heading not required.)

Instructions regarding War Diaries and Intelligence Summaries are contained in F.S. Regs., Part II. and the Staff Manual respectively. Title pages will be prepared in manuscript.

Place	Date	Hour	Summary of Events and Information	Remarks and references to Appendices
Field	7/6		Routine work.	App B
"	8/6		Routine work	App B
"	9/6		Routine work.	App B
"	10/6		Routine work	App B
"	11/6		Routine work	App B
"	12/6		Routine work. Railed 7 horses 1 mule to Tourges-Les-Aux	App B
"	13/6		Routine work	App B
"	14/6		Routine work. Railed 13 horses to Forges-les-Eaux	App B
"	15/6		Railed 5 horses to Forges-les-Eaux	App B
"	16/6		" 14 " " "	App B
"	17/6		Routine work	App B
"	18/6		Routine work; Railed 10 horses	App B
"	19/6		Railed 33 horses to Forges-les-Eaux	App B
"	20/6		Railed 8 horses " "	App B
"	21/6		Routine work	App B
"	22/6		Railed 25 horses 2 mules.	App B

T2134. Wt. W708—776. 500000. 4/15. Sir J. C. & S.

Army Form C. 2118.

WAR DIARY
or
INTELLIGENCE SUMMARY.
(Erase heading not required.)

Instructions regarding War Diaries and Intelligence Summaries are contained in F. S. Regs., Part II. and the Staff Manual respectively. Title pages will be prepared in manuscript.

Place	Date	Hour	Summary of Events and Information	Remarks and references to Appendices
Field	23/6		Routine work	RnB
"	24/6		Railed 31 horses	RnB
"	25/6		Established an advanced spot at BUS-les-ARTOIS.	RnB
"	26/6		Routine work	RnB
"	27/6		"	RnB
"	28/6		" Railed 23 horses and 3 mules	RnB
"	29/6		Routine work	RnB
"	30/6		Railed 20 horses to TORGES-les-EAUX.	RnB
"	1/7/16		Routine work	RnB
"	2/7/16		Railed 38 horses + 1 mule d˚ " "	RnB
"	3/7/16		Routine work	RnB
"	4/7/16		Railed 23 horses + 2 mules " "	RnB
"	5/7/16		Routine work	RnB
"	6/7/16		Railed 31 horses 10 mules to TORGES les-EAUX.	RnB
"	7/7/16		Routine work	RnB
"	8/7/16		Marched to HARDINVAL	RnB

D.A.G.
3rd Echelon

Herewith War Diary for the period from 22/5/16 to 22/6/16 please.

[signature] Capt. AVC
O.C. 41st Mob. Vety. Section

Confidential   Vol. V

War Diary
of
41st Mob. Vet. Section

1st July to 31st July,
1916.

Army Form C. 2118.

A.D.V.S.
No. 34/4.
Date. 1.9.16

51st Mobile Veterinary Section
No. Pin to Sel
Date 1.9.16

WAR DIARY
or
INTELLIGENCE SUMMARY
(Erase heading not required.)

Instructions regarding War Diaries and Intelligence Summaries are contained in F. S. Regs., Part II. and the Staff Manual respectively. Title pages will be prepared in manuscript.

Place	Date	Hour	Summary of Events and Information	Remarks and references to Appendices
Field	9/8		Marched to AUXI-LE-CHATEAU arriving 9pm Entrained 12 noon	PineS
	10/8		Detrained THIENNES 5.20 pm Marched to ST. FLORIS arriving 9 pm	PineS
	11/8		Billeted at LA HAIE	PineS
	12/8		Arranged with RTO LILLERS about sending sick horses to Base	PineS
	13/8		Admitted 60 horses	PineS
	14/8		Railed 48 horses to NEUF. CHATEL	PineS
"	15/8		Railed 49 " " "	PineS
"	16/8		" 17 " " "	PineS
"	17/8		Moved to PARADIS	PineS
"	18/8		Railed 22 horses	PineS
"	19/8		Routine work	PineS
"	20/8		" "	R.G. R.G.
"	21/8		Railed 47 hors, 1 mule to NEUF CHATEL	PineS
"	22/8		" 17 " and 3 cart by DAR 1st Army Routine work	PineS

T2134. Wt. W708—776. 500000. 4/15. Sir J. C. & S.

Army Form C. 2118.

WAR DIARY
or
INTELLIGENCE SUMMARY.
(Erase heading not required.)

Army Form.
A.D.V.S.
No. 31/14
Date 1.8.16.
31st DIVISION

51st Mobile Veterinary Section
No. M 441
Date 1.7.16

Instructions regarding War Diaries and Intelligence Summaries are contained in F.S. Regs., Part II. and the Staff Manual respectively. Title pages will be prepared in manuscript.

Place	Date	Hour	Summary of Events and Information	Remarks and references to Appendices
Field	23/7/16		Inspection of all kit nights etc.	R.C.B
"	24/7/16		Daily routine	Rout
"	25/7/16		Daily routine	Rout
"	26.7.16		Daily routine	RenB
"	27/7/16		Daily routine	RenB
"	28/7/16		18 horses and 4 mules sent by Range to NEUF CHATEL	RenB
"	29/7/16		Routine work	RenB
"	30/7/16		Routine work. Rifle inspection	RenB
"	31/7/16		Routine work	RenB

T2134. Wt. W708—776. 500000. 4/15. Sir J. C. & S.

Army Form C. 2118.

WAR DIARY
or
INTELLIGENCE SUMMARY.
(Erase heading not required.)

Instructions regarding War Diaries and Intelligence Summaries are contained in F.S. Regs., Part II. and the Staff Manual respectively. Title pages will be prepared in manuscript.

Place	Date	Hour	Summary of Events and Information	Remarks and references to Appendices
FIELD	1/16		Routine work. Sent 7 horses and 1 mule to Base Vety Hospital	RmS
"	2/16		Routine work	RmS
"	3/16		Routine work	RmS
"	4/16		Twenty one horses and 1 mule by Barge to St OMER	RmS
"	5/16		Twenty five " " " " to NEUFCHATEL	RmS
"	6/16		Routine work	RmS
"	7/16		Routine work	RmS
"	8/16		Ten horses and 1 mule evacuated by barge to St OMER	RmS
"	9/16		Routine work	RmS
"	10/16		4 horses by Barge to St OMER	RmS
"	11/16		Routine work	RmS
"	12/16		Routine work	RmS
"	13/16		Routine work	RmS
"	14/16		Routine work	RmS
"	15/16		Routine work	RmS
"	16/16		" "	RmS

R. W. Sampson Capt.
O.C. 41st Mob. Vety Sec.

Army Form C. 2118.

WAR DIARY
or
INTELLIGENCE SUMMARY.
(Erase heading not required.)

Instructions regarding War Diaries and Intelligence Summaries are contained in F. S. Regs., Part II. and the Staff Manual respectively. Title pages will be prepared in manuscript.

Place	Date	Hour	Summary of Events and Information	Remarks and references to Appendices
Field	17/16		Routine work	Ref
"	18/16		Eleven horses by Barge and 3 by rail to Base	Ref
"	19/16		Routine work	"
"	20/16		"	Ref 5
"	21/16		"	
"	22/16		Sent 8 horses by Barge to ST OMER	Ref
"	23/16		Routine work	Ref 3
"	24/16		Ten horses sent to ST OMER, four to NEUFCHATEL	Ref
"	25/16		Routine work	Ref 3
"	26/16		Two horses evacuated to NEUFCHATEL	Ref
"	27/16		Routine work	Ref 3
"	28/16		Routine work	Ref
"	29/16		Six horses evacuated by Barge to ST OMER	Ref
"	30/16		Routine work	Ref 3
"	31/16		Ten horses and two mules to ST OMER by Barge	Ref

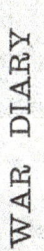

RW Beaufort Capt
OC 41st Mob. Vety Sec

Confidential. W V 7

War Diary.

Mobile Veterinary Section 31st Division

September 1916.

WAR DIARY
or
INTELLIGENCE SUMMARY.
(Erase heading not required.)

Place	Date	Hour	Summary of Events and Information	Remarks and references to Appendices
Field	1/2/16		Routine work	App 3
"	2/2/16		Routine work	App 3
"	3/2/16		Routine work	App 3
"	4/2/16		Routine work	App 3
"	5/2/16		7 sick animals evacuated to ST OMER	App 3
"	6/2/16		5 " " " NEUFCHATEL	App 3
"	7/2/16		9 " " " ST OMER	App 3
"	8/2/16		Routine work	App 3
"	9/2/16		Routine work	App 3
"	10/2/16		10 sick and saddlery inspection	App 3
"	11/2/16		Railed 16 horses to NEUFCHATEL	App 3
"	12/2/16		Routine work	App 3
"	13/2/16		Routine work	App 3
"	14/2/16		13 horses and 4 mules to ST OMER by Boys	App 3
"	15/2/16		Routine work	App 3
"	16/2/16		Routine work	App 3

R.A. Beaufort Capt
RC 4th Mob Vety Sec

Army Form C. 2118.

WAR DIARY
or
INTELLIGENCE SUMMARY.
(Erase heading not required.)

Instructions regarding War Diaries and Intelligence Summaries are contained in F. S. Regs., Part II. and the Staff Manual respectively. Title pages will be prepared in manuscript.

Place	Date	Hour	Summary of Events and Information	Remarks and references to Appendices
FIELD	17/16		Routine work. Inspection of kit, saddlery and arms	Ref B
"	18/16		Routine work	Ref B
"	19/16		Routine work	Ref B
"	20/16		Two horses to NEUFCHATEL	Ref B
"	21/16		Two horses evacuated to NEUFCHATEL and 3 mules	Ref B
"	22/16		Moved to LOCON	Ref B
"	23/16		Routine work	Ref B
"	24/16		1 horse to NEUFCHATEL	Ref B
"	25/16		Routine work	Ref B
"	26/16		Routine work	Ref B
"	27/16		Routine work	Ref B
"	28/16		Eighteen horses & 1 mule to ST OMER by charge	Ref B
"	29/16		Routine work	Ref B
"	30/16		Routine work	Ref B

R Rutherford Capt.
O.C. 41st Mob. Vety Sec

Confidential

Volume 8

War Diary

41st Mobile Veterinary Section   31st Division

October 1916.

Army Form C. 2118.

WAR DIARY
or
INTELLIGENCE SUMMARY.
(Erase heading not required.)

Instructions regarding War Diaries and Intelligence Summaries are contained in F.S. Regs., Part II. and the Staff Manual respectively. Title pages will be prepared in manuscript.

Vol 8

Place	Date	Hour	Summary of Events and Information	Remarks and references to Appendices
Field	1/10		Routine work. Inspection of kit, arms and saddlery	App B
"	2/10		Routine work	App B
"	3/10		9 animals evacuated by Barge to St OMER	App B
"	4/10		Routine work	App B
"	5/10		23 animals by Barge to St. OMER	App B
"	6/10		Routine work	App B
"	7/10		"	App B
"	8/10		"	App B
"	9/10		Marched to LILLERS and entrained	App B
"	10/10		Detrained at DOULLENS and marched to Villeks at TERRAMESNIL	App B
"	11/10		Routine work	App B
"	12/10		"	App B
"	13/10		"	App B
"	14/10		Railed 22 horses and 1 mule to ABBEVILLE	App B
"	15/10		Routine work	App B
"	16/10		"	App B

W H Bird Lieut
O.C. 41st Mobile Vety. Section.

WAR DIARY or INTELLIGENCE SUMMARY.

Army Form C. 2118.

Instructions regarding War Diaries and Intelligence Summaries are contained in F.S. Regs., Part II. and the Staff Manual respectively. Title pages will be prepared in manuscript.

(Erase heading not required.)

Place	Date	Hour	Summary of Events and Information	Remarks and references to Appendices
Field.	17/10		Routine work	AWM
"	18/10		Railed 24 sick animals to FORGES-les-EAUX. Moved to AUTHIE	AWM
"	19/10		Routine work	AWM
"	20/10		"	AWM
"	21/10		Railed 16 horses	AWM
"	22/10		Routine work	AWM
"	23/10		26 sick railed to ABBEVILLE	AWM
"	24/10		Formed an advance party at SAILLY au BOIS.	AWM
AUTHIE	25.10.16		Capt Bamford A.V.C. nck. Major Matthews A.V.C. A.V.R. over charge 20 animals railed to ABBEVILLE	AWM
"	26.10.16		Routine work	AWM
"	27/10		16 animals evacuated to ABBEVILLE. Capt Butcher A.V.C. took over charge. Temporary.	AWM
"	28/10		Routine work.	AWM
"	29/10		Inspected by D.V.S. Reserve Army. Routine work	AWM
"	30/10		8 animals evacuated to ABBEVILLE	AWM
"	31/10		Railed 8 horses to ABBEVILLE	AWM

G.H. Butcher Capt. A.V.C.
O/c 41st Mobile Vety. Section

Confidential

Volume XI

No 9

War Diary.

41st Mobile Veterinary Section

November 1916.

Army Form C. 2118.

WAR DIARY
or
INTELLIGENCE SUMMARY.
(Erase heading not required.)

Instructions regarding War Diaries and Intelligence Summaries are contained in F.S. Regs, Part II. and the Staff Manual respectively. Title pages will be prepared in manuscript.

Place	Date	Hour	Summary of Events and Information	Remarks and references to Appendices
AUTHIE	1/7/16		Routine work.	
"	2/7/16		Routine work	
"	3/7/16		Railed to ABBEVILLE 10 horses & 7 mules.	
"	4/7/16		Routine work.	
"	5/7/16		Railed to ABBEVILLE 24 horses. The advanced posts at SAILLY &	
"	6/7/16		I.N.C.O & 2 men was ordered to rejoin the H.Q. 2nd M.V.S.	
"	7/7/16		Railed to ABBEVILLE 23 horses	
"	8/7/16		Routine work	
"	9/7/16		Routine work	
"	10/7/16		Railed to ABBEVILLE 8 animals. Inspected by D.D.V.S 6th Army	
"	11/7/16		Routine work	
"	12/7/16		Railed to ABBEVILLE 34 animals.	
"			Railed to ABBEVILLE 8 animals. Re-established advanced Posts — at J.16.6.8.3 (Sheet 57 D)	
"	13/7/16		Routine work	
"	14/7/16		Railed to ABBEVILLE 37 horses.	

T2134. Wt. W708—776. 500000. 4/15. Sir J. C. & S.

Army Form C. 2118.

WAR DIARY
or
INTELLIGENCE SUMMARY.
(Erase heading not required.)

Instructions regarding War Diaries and Intelligence Summaries are contained in F. S. Regs., Part II. and the Staff Manual respectively. Title pages will be prepared in manuscript.

Place	Date	Hour	Summary of Events and Information	Remarks and references to Appendices
FIELD	15/6		Took over from Capt BUTCHER. Railed 35 sick animals to ABBEVILLE	Pub 3
"	16/6		Railed 23 sick animals to ABBEVILLE	Pub 3
"	17/6		Routine work	Pub 3
"	18/6		Railed 33 sick animals to ABBEVILLE.	Pub 3
"	19/6		" 32 " " "	Pub 3
"	20/6		" 48 " " "	Pub 3
"	21/6		" 46 " " "	Pub 3
"	22/6		" 47 " " " Advanced post at SAILLY withdrawn.	Pub 3
"	23/6		" 54 " " "	Pub 3
"	24/6		" 22 " " "	Pub 3
"	25/6		" 16 " " "	Pub 3
"	26/6		Routine work	Pub 3
"	27/6		Routine work	Pub 3
"	28/6		Railed 29 sick animals to ABBEVILLE	Pub 3
"	29/6		Routine work	Pub 3
"	30/6		Railed 19 sick animals to ABBEVILLE	Pub 3

R W Bampton
Capt N&Y
OC 1st Mob: Vety Sec

Confidential

Volume II
Vol 10

War Diary.

41st Mobile Veterinary Section

December 1916.

Army Form C. 2118.

WAR DIARY
or
INTELLIGENCE SUMMARY.
(Erase heading not required.)

Instructions regarding War Diaries and Intelligence Summaries are contained in F.S. Regs., Part II. and the Staff Manual respectively. Title pages will be prepared in manuscript.

Place	Date	Hour	Summary of Events and Information	Remarks and references to Appendices
FIELD	1/12/16		Routine work	Pur R
"	2/12/16		Routine work	Pur R
"	3/12/16		Handed over to Capt Butcher ACR	Pur R
"	4/12/16		23 animals evacuated to ABBEVILLE	6/443
"	5/12/16		Routine work	4/443
"	6/12/16		25 animals evacuated to ABBEVILLE	6/443
"	7/12/16		Collected 1 animal at FAMECHON	4/443
"	8/12/16		10 animals evacuated to ABBEVILLE	6/443
"	9/12/16		Collected 1 animal at ORVILLE	6/443
"	10/12/16		Routine work	4/443
"	11/12/16		22 animals evacuated to ABBEVILLE	6/443
"	12/12/16		Routine work	6/443
"	13/12/16		Routine work	6/443
"	14/12/16		Routine work	6/443
"	15/12/16		17 animals evacuated to ABBEVILLE	6/443
"	16/12/16		Routine work	6/443

Rwd Sanford Capt
OC 41st Mob. Vety Sec

Army Form C. 2118.

WAR DIARY
or
INTELLIGENCE SUMMARY.
(Erase heading not required.)

Instructions regarding War Diaries and Intelligence Summaries are contained in F. S. Regs., Part II. and the Staff Manual respectively. Title pages will be prepared in manuscript.

Place	Date	Hour	Summary of Events and Information	Remarks and references to Appendices
FIELD	17/12/16		Routine work	Pub B
"	18/12/16		"	Pub B
"	19/12/16		"	Pub B
"	20/12/16		"	Pub B
"	21/12/16		Railed 28 sick to ABBEVILLE	Pub B
"	22/12/16		Routine work	Pub B
"	23/12/16		"	Pub B
"	24/12/16		Railed 12 sick to ABBEVILLE	Pub B
"	25/12/16		Xmas day	Pub B
"	26/12/16		Railed 21 " "	Pub B
"	27/12/16		Routine work	Pub B
"	28/12/16		Routine work	Pub B
"	29/12/16		Routine work	Pub B
"	30/12/16		Railed 25 sick animals to ABBEVILLE	Pub B
"	31/12/16		Routine work	Pub B

Paul Bamford Capt
OC 41st Mob: Vety Sec

Confidential

Volume XI

Vol XI

War Diary

41st Mobile Veterinary Section   31st Division

January 1917.

Army Form C. 2118

WAR DIARY
or
INTELLIGENCE SUMMARY
(Erase heading not required.)

Instructions regarding War Diaries and Intelligence Summaries are contained in F.S. Regs., Part II. and the Staff Manual respectively. Title Pages will be prepared in manuscript.

Place	Date	Hour	Summary of Events and Information	Remarks and references to Appendices
FIELD	1/7		Holiday	Routine
"	2/7		Thirty sick railed to ABBEVILLE	Routine
"	3/7		Routine work	Routine
"	4/7		Railed 19 sick to ABBEVILLE	Routine
"	5/7		" 12 " "	Routine
"	6/7		" 16 " "	Routine
"	7/7		" 26 " "	Routine
"	8/7		Routine work	Routine
"	9/7		"	Routine
"	10/7		Railed 36 sick to ABBEVILLE	Routine
"	11/7		Routine work	Routine
"	12/7		Marched to BEAUVAL	Routine
"	13/7		Routine work	Routine
"	14/7		"	Routine

Army Form C. 2118

WAR DIARY
or
INTELLIGENCE SUMMARY
(Erase heading not required.)

Instructions regarding War Diaries and Intelligence Summaries are contained in F.S. Regs., Part II. and the Staff Manual respectively. Title Pages will be prepared in manuscript.

Place	Date	Hour	Summary of Events and Information	Remarks and references to Appendices
FIELD	15/7		Routine work	Pub
"	16/7		" "	Pub
"	17/7		" "	Pub
"	18/7		" "	Pub
"	19/7		17 sick railed to ABBEVILLE	Pub
"	20/7		Routine work	Pub
"	21/7		" "	Pub
"	22/7		Moved to BERNAVILLE. Railed 9 sick animals	Pub
"	23/7		Routine work	Pub
"	24/7		" "	Pub
"	25/7		" "	Pub
"	26/7		Railed 41 sick animals to ABBEVILLE	Pub

Army Form C. 2118

WAR DIARY
or
INTELLIGENCE SUMMARY
(Erase heading not required.)

Place	Date	Hour	Summary of Events and Information	Remarks and references to Appendices
FIELD	27/7		Routine work	PmB
"	28/7		"	PmB
"	29/7		"	PmB
"	30/7		"	PmB
"	31/7		Railed 21 mules to ABBEVILLE	PmB

Railed very few

R.W. Sandford
Capt
OC 41st Mob. Vet Sec.

Confidential

Volume XIV

9/1/12

War Diary.

41st Mobile Veterinary Section) 31st Division

February 1917.

WAR DIARY
or
INTELLIGENCE SUMMARY
(Erase heading not required.)

Army Form C. 2118

Place	Date	Hour	Summary of Events and Information	Remarks and references to Appendices
FIELD	1/7		Routine work	Reub
"	2/7		"	Reub
"	3/7		"	Reub
"	4/7		"	Reub
"	5/7		"	Reub
"	6/7		"	Reub
"	7/7		"	Reub
"	8/7		"	
"	9/7		"	
"	10/7		"	
"	11/7		"	
"	12/7		Twenty two animals evacuated	

G.H.Mueller Capt AVC
O.C. 1st mobile Vety Section

WAR DIARY
or
INTELLIGENCE SUMMARY

Army Form C. 2118.

Instructions regarding War Diaries and Intelligence Summaries are contained in F.S. Regs., Part II. and the Staff Manual respectively. Title Pages will be prepared in manuscript.

31st DIVIS.

Place	Date	Hour	Summary of Events and Information	Remarks and references to Appendices
FIELD	13/2/17		Sixteen animals evacuated	6/4/3
"	14/2/17		Routine work	9/4/4
"	15/2/17		"	9/4/4
"	16/2/17		" Taken over charge of J. & V.S. Section	J.P.S.Bishaustelle 9.3.9
"	17/2/17		Capt. H. BUTCHER A.V.C. took over charge of 41 M.V.S. from Capt. Little A.V.C.	9/3.9
"	18/2/17		Railed to ABBEVILLE 19 animals – Routine work	9/4/3
"	19/2/17		Routine work	6/4/3
"	20/2/17		Routine work – Railed 6 animals to ABBEVILLE	C/4/3
"	21/2/17		Marched to AUTHIE	9/4/3
"	22/2/17		Routine work	9/4/3

C.H.Butcher Capt A.V.
O.C. 41st Mobile Vety. Section

Army Form C. 2118

WAR DIARY
or
INTELLIGENCE SUMMARY
(Erase heading not required.)

Place	Date	Hour	Summary of Events and Information	Remarks and references to Appendices
FIELD	23/7		Routine work	G/WB
"	24/7		Routine work	G/WB
"	25/7		Routine work	G/WB
"	26/7		Routine work	G/WB
"	27/7		Routine work	G/WB
"	28/7		Railed 40 animals to ABBEVILLE.	G/WB

G M Burcher
OC 41st Mobile Vety Station
Canb. ave.

Confidential

Volume XV

VK/3

War Diary.

41. Mobile Veterinary Section.

31st. Division.

March 1917.

Army Form C. 2118

WAR DIARY
or
INTELLIGENCE SUMMARY
(Erase heading not required.)

Instructions regarding War Diaries and Intelligence Summaries are contained in F. S. Regs., Part II. and the Staff Manual respectively. Title Pages will be prepared in manuscript.

Place	Date	Hour	Summary of Events and Information	Remarks and references to Appendices
In the Field	1/3/17		Routine work	G.W.B.
"	2/3/17		Evacuated 22 animals to ABBEVILLE	G.W.B.
"	3/3/17		Sent 1 N.C.O. & 14 vet hveo to ACHEUX to bring in pack saddles for ordnance	G.W.B.
"	4/3/17		Routine work	G.W.B.
"	5/3/17		Evacuated 11 animals to ABBEVILLE	G.W.B.
"	6/3/17		Routine work	G.W.B.
"	7/3/17		Evacuated 16 animals to ABBEVILLE	G.W.B.
"	8/3/17		Capt Renshaw 2nd i/c took A Section from Capt Butcher A.V.C. proceeding on 10 days leave	J.B.J.
"	9/3/17		Routine work	J.B.J.
"	10/3/17		"	J.B.J.
"	11/3/17		"	J.B.J.

WAR DIARY or INTELLIGENCE SUMMARY

Army Form C. 2118

Place	Date	Hour	Summary of Events and Information	Remarks and references to Appendices
FIELD	12/3/17		Evacuated 32 sick animals to ABBEVILLE	J.B.9
"	13/3/17		Routine work	J.B.9
"	14/3/17		" "	J.B.9
"	15/3/17		" "	J.B.9
"	16/3/17		Evacuated 41 sick animals to ABBEVILLE	J.B.9
"	17/3/17		Routine work	J.B.9
"	18/3/17		" "	J.B.9
"	19/3/17		Evacuated 14 horses to ABBEVILLE	J.M.11
"	20/3/17		Marched from AUTHIE to BOUQUE MAISON — Capt Butcher assumed command of Section	J.M.13
"	21/3/17		" from BOUQUE MAISON to GUINE COURT	J.M.13

Army Form C. 2118

WAR DIARY
or
INTELLIGENCE SUMMARY
(Erase heading not required.)

Instructions regarding War Diaries and Intelligence Summaries are contained in F. S. Regs., Part II. and the Staff Manual respectively. Title Pages will be prepared in manuscript.

Place	Date	Hour	Summary of Events and Information	Remarks and references to Appendices
FIELD	22/3/17		Marched from Quinecourt to Pressy-les-Pernes	
"	23/3/17		Rested	
"	24/3/17		Marched from Pressy-les-Pernes to Laires	
"	25/3/17		Marched from Laires to La Haye (near Floris)	
"	26/3/17		Routine work	
"	27/3/17		Routine work	
"	28/3/17		Routine work	
"	29/3/17		Routine work	
"	30/3/17		Routine work	
"	31/3/17		Routine work	

Capt. R.V.C.
O.C. 41st Mob. Vet. Sec.

Confidential

Volume XVI

WD/4

War Diary.

41st Mobile Veterinary Section 31st Division

April 1917.

Army Form C. 2118

WAR DIARY
or
INTELLIGENCE SUMMARY
(Erase heading not required.)

Instructions regarding War Diaries and Intelligence Summaries are contained in F.S. Regs., Part II. and the Staff Manual respectively. Title Pages will be prepared in manuscript.

Place	Date	Hour	Summary of Events and Information	Remarks and references to Appendices
In the Field	1/4/17		Routine work	
"	2/4/17		Routine work	
"	3/4/17		Evacuated 15 animals to NEUFCHATEL	
"	4/4/17		Routine work	
"	5/4/17		Routine work	
"	6/4/17		Routine work	
"	7/4/17		Evacuated 6 animals to NEUFCHATEL	
"	8/4/17		Marched to ZAPUGNOY	
"	9/4/17		Routine work	
"	10/4/17		Routine work	

WAR DIARY or INTELLIGENCE SUMMARY

Army Form C. 2118

Place	Date	Hour	Summary of Events and Information	Remarks and references to Appendices
In the Field	Apr 11		Routine Work	
	12		Evacuated 2 animals to Base through 1/ Last Lancs M.V.S at BETHUNE	
	13		Routine Work	
	14		Evacuated 2 animals to "Base this" 1/ Last Lancs M.V.S. - the section marched	
			to LA COMTÉ via BRUAY	
	15		Routine Work	
	16		Routine Work	
	17		Routine Work	
	18		Routine Work	
	19		Routine Work	
	20		Evacuated 9 animals to NEUFCHATEL	
	21		Routine Work	
	22		Routine Work	

Army Form C. 2118

WAR DIARY
or
INTELLIGENCE SUMMARY

(Erase heading not required.)

Instructions regarding War Diaries and Intelligence Summaries are contained in F.S. Regs., Part II. and the Staff Manual respectively. Title Pages will be prepared in manuscript.

Place	Date	Hour	Summary of Events and Information	Remarks and references to Appendices
In the Field	23/7/17		Routine work	5/17/13
"	24/7/17		Routine work	5/17/13
"	25/7/17		Routine work	5/17/13
"	26/7/17		Routine work	5/17/13
"	27/7/17		Evacuated 14 animals to NEUFCHATEL	5/17/13
"	28/7/17		Routine work	5/17/13
"	29/7/17		Routine work	5/17/13
"	30/7/17		Marched to MARŒUIL. Made over 4 animals to No.3 C.L. 63rd Div Vet. begun marching	5/17/13

G.W. Buechli
Capt AVC
O/C. 41st M.V.S.

Confidential

Volume XVII

Vol 15

War Diary.

41st Mobile Vet: Section

31st Division

May 1917.

WAR DIARY
or
INTELLIGENCE SUMMARY

Army Form C. 2118

Place	Date	Hour	Summary of Events and Information	Remarks and references to Appendices
In the Field	1/5/17		Evacuated 49 animals to No 3 M.V.S. at ECOUVRES	GMc3
"	2/5/17		Evacuated 14 animals to No 3 M.V.S at ECOUVRES. 5 Collected	GMc3
			an advanced post at the STEARINERIE, St Nicholas (NCO & 10C) 2.11.17.	GMc3
"	3/5/17		Routine work. 1 animal destroyed	GMc3
"	4/5/17		Evacuated 29 animals to No 3 M.V.S at ECOUVRES	GMc3
"	5/5/17		Evacuated 35 arrivals to No 3 M.V.S at ECOUVRES	GMc3
"	6/5/17		Evacuated 21 animals to No 3 M.V.S	GMc3
"	7/5/17		Evacuated 20 animals to No 3 M.V.S. 1 animal destroyed	GMc3
"	8/5/17		Evacuated 39 animals to No 3 M.V.S	GMc3
"	9/5/17		Routine work. Visited advanced post at St Nicholas	GMc3
"	10/5/17		Evacuated 31 animals to No 3 M.V.S	GMc3

Army Form C. 2118

WAR DIARY
or
INTELLIGENCE SUMMARY

(Erase heading not required.)

Instructions regarding War Diaries and Intelligence Summaries are contained in F. S. Regs., Part II. and the Staff Manual respectively. Title Pages will be prepared in manuscript.

Place	Date	Hour	Summary of Events and Information	Remarks and references to Appendices
In the Field	11-5-17		Evacuated 31 animals to No 3 M.V.S. at ECOIVRES	GWS
"	12-5-17		Evacuated 20 animals to No 3 M.V.S. Withdrew advanced post from S. NICHOLAS	GWS
"	13-5-17		Evacuated 26 animals to No 3 M.V.S. at ECOIVRES	GWS
"	14-5-17		Evacuated 80 animals to No 3 M.V.S.	GWS
"	15-5-17		Evacuated 5-9 animals to No 3 M.V.S. 1 animal destroyed	GWS
"	16-5-17		Evacuated 23 animals to No 3 M.V.S.	GWS
"	17-5-17		Routine work	GWS
"	18-5-17		Evacuated 49 animals to ECOIVRES 1 animal destroyed	GWS
"	19-5-17		Routine work	GWS
"	20-5-17		Evacuated 26 animals to No 3 M.V.S. at ECOIVRES - Inspected by D.D.V.S.	GWS
"	21-5-17		Evacuated 3 horses & 1 mule to No 3 at ECOIVRES	GWS

Army Form C. 2118

WAR DIARY
or
INTELLIGENCE SUMMARY
(Erase heading not required.)

Instructions regarding War Diaries and Intelligence Summaries are contained in F. S. Regs., Part II. and the Staff Manual respectively. Title Pages will be prepared in manuscript.

Place	Date	Hour	Summary of Events and Information	Remarks and references to Appendices
In the Field	22-5-17		Evacuated 29 animals to N⁰ 3 M.V.S. at ECOIVRES	JHB
"	23-5-17		Routine work	JHB
"	24-5-17		Evacuated 12 animals to N⁰ 3 M.V.S. at ECOIVRES	JHB
"	25-5-17		Routine work	JHB
"	26-5-17		Evacuated 8 animals to N⁰ 3 M.V.S. at ECOIVRES	JHB
"	27-5-17		Routine work	JHB
"	28-5-17		Routine work	JHB
"	29-5-17		Evacuated 11 animals to N⁰ 3 M.V.S. at ECOIVRES 1 animal destroyed	JHB
"	30		Routine work	JHB
"	31-5-17		Evacuated 12 animals to N⁰ 3 M.V.S. at ECOIVRES	JHB

In the Field
31/5/17

J.H. Butcher
Capt. A.V.C.
O.C. #1 st Mobile Vety. Section

Confidential

Volume XVIII

WO 16

War Diary.

41st Mobile Veterinary Section 31st Division

June 1917

WAR DIARY
or
INTELLIGENCE SUMMARY

(Erase heading not required.)

Army Form C. 2118

Place	Date	Hour	Summary of Events and Information	Remarks and references to Appendices
FIELD	1/6/17		Routine work	
"	2-6-17		Evacuated 4 animals to No 3 M.V.S at ECOIVRES	
"	3-6-17		Evacuated 11 animals to No 3 M.V.S at ECOIVRES	
"	4-6-17		Evacuated 7 animals to No 3 M.V.S at ECOIVRES	
"	5-6-17		Routine work	
"	6-6-17		Routine work	
"	7-6-17		Evacuated 10 animals to No 3 M.V.S at ECOIVRES	
"	8-6-17		Evacuated 8 animals to No 3 M.V.S at ECOIVRES	
"	9-6-17		Routine work	
"	10-6-17		Routine work	
"	11-6-17		Evacuated 11 Animals to No 3 M.V.S at ECOIVRES	
"	12-6-17		Routine work	

Army Form C. 2118

WAR DIARY
or
INTELLIGENCE SUMMARY
(Erase heading not required.)

Instructions regarding War Diaries and Intelligence Summaries are contained in F. S. Regs., Part II. and the Staff Manual respectively. Title Pages will be prepared in manuscript.

Place	Date	Hour	Summary of Events and Information	Remarks and references to Appendices
FIELD	13-6-17		Routine work	
"	14-6-17		Routine work	
"	15-6-17		Routine work	
"	16-6-17		Evacuated 6 animals to No 3 M.V.S at ECOIVRES	
"	17-6-17		Routine work. Evacuated 2 animals to No 3 M.V.S ECOIVRES	
"	18-6-17		Routine work	
"	19-6-17		Routine work	
"	20-6-17		Evacuated 6 animals to NEUF CHATEL	
"	21-6-17		Routine work	
"	22-6-17		Routine work	
"	23-6-17		Routine work - Inspected by A.D.V.S. XIII Corps	
"	24-6-17		MAJOR MATTHEWS A.V.C. took over from Capt DUTCHER who goes on leave	

Army Form C. 2118

WAR DIARY
or
INTELLIGENCE SUMMARY
(Erase heading not required.)

Instructions regarding War Diaries and Intelligence Summaries are contained in F. S. Regs., Part II. and the Staff Manual respectively. Title Pages will be prepared in manuscript.

Place	Date	Hour	Summary of Events and Information	Remarks and references to Appendices
FIELD	25.6.17		Routine work	ACM
"	26.6.17		Routine work	ACM
"	27.6.17		Routine work	ACM
"	28.6.17		Routine work	ACM
"	29.6.17		Routine work	ACM
"	30.6.17		Routine work	ACM
			A.C.Matthews Major AVC Com 41 Mot Vet Sec	

1875 Wt. W593/826 1,000,000 4/15 J.B.C. & A. A.D.S.S./Forms/C. 2118.

Confidential

Volume XIX

War Diary.

41st Mobile Veterinary Section   31st Division

July 1917

WAR DIARY
or
INTELLIGENCE SUMMARY

(Erase heading not required.)

41 Motor Vety Section

Place	Date	Hour	Summary of Events and Information	Remarks and references to Appendices
Field	1-7-17		Routine work	RCM
"	2-7-17		Routine work	RCM
"	3-7-17		One case of Stomatitis Contagiosa. Section ordered by DADVS to take no more sick nor outbreak over sick animals arriving to to sick to other Mot Vet section in the neighbourhood	RCM
"	4-7-17		Atos animal seen today from Roumania caused by severe running P.M showed no signs of collapses. Precautions taken.	ACM
"	5-7-17		Routine work - Capt BUTCHER returned from 10 days leave & resumed charge	GMC
"	6-7-17		Evacuated 11 animals to Vety CHATEL	GMC
"	7-7-17		Section marched back to cut at MAROEUIL	GMC
"	8-7-17		Routine work	GMC

Army Form C. 2118

WAR DIARY
or
INTELLIGENCE SUMMARY

(Erase heading not required.)

41st Mob. Vet. Sec.

[Stamp: 41st Mobile Veterinary Section No. M3/6/8 Date 1.8.17]

Instructions regarding War Diaries and Intelligence Summaries are contained in F.S. Regs., Part II. and the Staff Manual respectively. Title Pages will be prepared in manuscript.

Place	Date	Hour	Summary of Events and Information	Remarks and references to Appendices
Field	9-7-17		Routine work. A.D.V.S. XIII Corps visited Section	GWB
"	10-7-17		Inspected by D.D.V.S. 1st Army	GWB
"	11-7-17		Routine work	GWB
"	12-7-17		Evacuated 19 animals to NEUFCHATEL, also 1 remount on arrival	GWB
"	13-7-17		Routine work	GWB
"	14-7-17		Routine work	GWB
"	15-7-17		Evacuated 4 animals to NEUFCHATEL	GWB
"	16-7-17		Routine work	GWB
"	17-7-17		Evacuated 2 animals to NEUFCHATEL	GWB
"	18-7-17		Routine work	GWB
"	19-7-17		A.D.V.S. XIII Corps inspected Section	GWB
"	20-7-17		Evacuated 20 animals to NEUFCHATEL	GWB
"	21-7-17		Routine work	GWB
"	22-7-17		Routine work	GWB
"	23-7-17		Routine work	GWB

Army Form C. 2118

WAR DIARY
or
INTELLIGENCE SUMMARY
(Erase heading not required.)

Instructions regarding War Diaries and Intelligence Summaries are contained in F. S. Regs., Part II. and the Staff Manual respectively. Title Pages will be prepared in manuscript.

Place	Date	Hour	Summary of Events and Information	Remarks and references to Appendices
In the Field	24.7.17		Evacuated 7 animals to NEUFCHATEL	GHB
"	25.7.17		Marched to (Map 57A) A.14.c.	GHB
"	26.7.17		Routine work	GHB
"	27.7.17		Evacuated 12 animals to NEUFCHATEL	GHB
"	28.7.17		Moved to camp at (Map 57A) A.8.c.6.4.	GHB
"	29.7.17		Routine work	GHB
"	30.7.17		Routine work	GHB
"	31.7.17		Routine work	GHB

In the Field
1-8-17.

G.H. Butcher
Captain.
O.C. 41st Mn. V.S.

Confidential

Volume XX
VA 18

War Diary.

41st Mobile Veterinary Section

31st Division

6 August 1917.

WAR DIARY
or
INTELLIGENCE SUMMARY

Army Form C. 2118

Place	Date	Hour	Summary of Events and Information	Remarks and references to Appendices
Field	1-8-17		Evacuated 20 animals to NEUFCHATEL from FEUR18 railhead	
"	2-8-17		Routine work	
"	3-8-17		Routine work	
"	4-8-17		Routine work	
"	5-8-17		Routine work	
"	6-8-17		Evacuated 22 animals to NEUF CHATEL	
"	7-8-17		Routine work	
"	8-8-17		Evacuated 30 animals to NEUFCHATEL	
"	9-8-17		Routine work	
"	10-8-17		Evacuated 14 animals to NEUF CHATEL	
"	11-8-17		Routine work	

Army Form C. 2118

WAR DIARY
or
INTELLIGENCE SUMMARY

(Erase heading not required.)

Instructions regarding War Diaries and Intelligence Summaries are contained in F. S. Regs., Part II. and the Staff Manual respectively. Title Pages will be prepared in manuscript.

Place	Date	Hour	Summary of Events and Information	Remarks and references to Appendices
In the Field	12-8-17		Routine work	
"	13-8-17		Routine work	
"	14-8-17		Routine work	
"	15-8-17		Evacuated 32 animals - Commenced building winter clothing.	
"	16-8-17		Routine work.	
"	17-8-17		Routine work	
"	18-8-17		Routine work	
"	19-8-17		Routine work	
"	20-8-17		Routine work	
"	21-8-17		Routine work	
"	22-8-17		Routine work	
"	23-8-17		Routine work	
"	24-8-17		Routine work - Evacuated 16 animals to Base.	
"	25-8-17		Routine work	

Army Form C. 2118

WAR DIARY
or
INTELLIGENCE SUMMARY
(Erase heading not required.)

Instructions regarding War Diaries and Intelligence Summaries are contained in F.S. Regs., Part II. and the Staff Manual respectively. Title Pages will be prepared in manuscript.

Place	Date	Hour	Summary of Events and Information	Remarks and references to Appendices
In the Field	26-8-17		Routine work	G.642
"	27-8-17		Routine work	G.643
"	28-8-17		Routine work	G.644
"	29-8-17		Routine work	G.645
"	30-8-17		Routine work	G.646
"	31-8-17		Evacuated 15 animals to the Base	G.647

In the Field
1-9-17.

G.M. Butcher
Capt. A.V.C.
O.C. 41st Mob. Vet. Sec.

Confidential.

Volume XXI

Vol 19

War Diary.

31st Division

41st Mobile Vet: Section

September 1917.

Army Form C. 2118

WAR DIARY
or
INTELLIGENCE SUMMARY

(Erase heading not required.)

Instructions regarding War Diaries and Intelligence Summaries are contained in F. S. Regs., Part II. and the Staff Manual respectively. Title Pages will be prepared in manuscript.

4/5 M.V.S.

Place	Date	Hour	Summary of Events and Information	Remarks and references to Appendices
In the Field	1-9-17		Routine Work	
"	2-9-17		Routine Work	
"	3-9-17		Routine Work	
"	4-9-17		Routine Work	
"	5-9-17		Routine Work - Evacuated 11 animals to Base	
"	6-9-17		Moved Camp to A20 a 9.6. Sheet 37B. (ECURIE)	
"	7-9-17		Routine Work	
"	8-9-17		Routine Work	
"	x9-9-17		Routine Work	
"	10-9-17		Routine Work	
"	11-9-17		Routine Work	
"	12-9-17		Evacuated 10 animals to Base	

WAR DIARY
or
INTELLIGENCE SUMMARY 41st M.V.S.

Army Form C. 2118

Place	Date	Hour	Summary of Events and Information	Remarks and references to Appendices
Field	13-9-17		Routine Work	
"	14-9-17		Routine Work	
"	15-9-17		Routine Work	
"	16-9-17		Routine Work	
"	17-9-17		Evacuated 14 animals to Base	
"	18-9-17		Routine Work	
"	19-9-17		Routine Work	
"	20-9-17		Routine Work	
"	21-9-17		Routine Work	
"	22-9-17		Evacuated 13 animals to Base	
"	23-9-17		Routine Work	
"	24-9-17		Routine Work	
"	25-9-17		Routine Work	
"	26-9-17		Routine Work	

WAR DIARY or INTELLIGENCE SUMMARY

Army Form C. 2118

41st M.V.S.

Place	Date	Hour	Summary of Events and Information	Remarks and references to Appendices
Field	27-9-17		Routine Work	
"	28-9-17		Routine Work	
"	29-9-17		Evacuated 18 animals to Base	
"	30-9-17		Routine Work	

W.H. Butcher Capt A.V.C.
O.C. 41st M.V.S.

"Confidential"

Volume X"
WM 20

War Diary.

41st Mobile. Vet. Section 31st Division

October 1917.

Army Form C. 2118

WAR DIARY
or
INTELLIGENCE SUMMARY
(Erase heading not required.)

Instructions regarding War Diaries and Intelligence Summaries are contained in F. S. Regs., Part II. and the Staff Manual respectively. Title Pages will be prepared in manuscript.

41st M.V.S.

Place	Date	Hour	Summary of Events and Information	Remarks and references to Appendices
Fraed	1-10-17		Routine work	G/LES
"	2-10-17		Routine work	J/LES
"	3-10-17		Routine work	J/LES
"	4-10-17		Evacuated 13 animals to Base	J/LES
"	5-10-17		Routine work	J/LES
"	6-10-17		Routine work	J/LES
"	7-10-17		Routine work	J/LES
"	8-10-17		Routine work. Evacuated 14 animals to Base	J/LES
"	9-10-17		Evacuated 8 animals (last) to Base	J/LES
"	10.10.17		Routine work	G/LES
"	11.10.17		Routine work	J/LES
"	12.10.17		Routine work	J/LES
"	13.10.17		Evacuated 9 animals to Base	J/LES
"	14.10.17		Routine work	G/LES

1875 Wt. W593/826 1,000,000 4/15 J.B.C. & A. A.D.S.S./Forms/C. 2118.

WAR DIARY
or
INTELLIGENCE SUMMARY

Army Form C. 2118

41st Mob. Vet. Sec.

Place	Date	Hour	Summary of Events and Information	Remarks and references to Appendices
Field	15-10-17		Routine work	App.
"	16-10-17		13 men KOYLI attach'd for duty sent on to R.E's Roclincourt	App.
"	17-10-17		8 men (reinforcement) arrived from No. 8 Vet. Hospital	App.
"	18-10-17		10 animals evacuated to Base	App.
"	19-10-17		Routine work	App.
"	20-10-17		Routine work - Capt. Boulter proceed on 10 days leave to England	App.
"	21-10-17		Capt. Bryges assumes command of sect. during his absence	App.
"	22-10-17		Routine work	App.
"	23-10-17		Routine work	App.
"	24-10-17		Routine work	App.
"	25-10-17		Routine work	App.
"	26-10-17		Routine work	App.
"	27-10-17		10 Animals evacuated to Base	App.
"	28-10-17		Routine work	App.

WAR DIARY or INTELLIGENCE SUMMARY

Army Form C. 2118

Place	Date	Hour	Summary of Events and Information	Remarks and references to Appendices
Fulli	29/10/17		Routine work	
"	30/10/17		Routine work	
"	31/10/17		Routine work	
"				

J.M. Bright Capt. A.V.C.
O.C. 41st Mobile Veterinary Section

Confidential

Volume XXIII

WA 21

War Diary.

No 1 Mobile Veterinary Section. 1st Division.

November 1917.

Army Form C. 2118

WAR DIARY
or
INTELLIGENCE SUMMARY   4 ᵗʰ M.V.S

(Erase heading not required.)

Place	Date	Hour	Summary of Events and Information	Remarks and references to Appendices
Field	1	11/17	Routine work	LAM
"	2	11/17	Routine work	LAM
"	3	11/17	Routine work - Resumed command of Sect. from Capt. BRIGHT AVC	GMS
"	4	11/17	Routine work	GMS
"	5	11/17	Routine work	GMS
"	6	11/17	Routine work	GMS
"	7	11/17	Routine work	GMS
"	8	11/17	Routine work	GMS
"	9	11/17	Evacuated 11 animals to Base	GMS
"	10	11/17	Routine work.	GMS
"	11	11/17	Inspected by W. Martin D.D.V.S 1ˢᵗ Army.	GMS

Army Form C. 2118

WAR DIARY
or
INTELLIGENCE SUMMARY 41st M.V.S.
(Erase heading not required.)

Place	Date	Hour	Summary of Events and Information	Remarks and references to Appendices
Field	12	/7	Evacuated 14 animals to Base	
"	13	/7	Routine work	
"	14	/7	Routine work	
"	15	/7	Routine work	
"	16	/7	Routine work	
"	17	/7	Evacuated 2 animals to Base	
"	18	/7	Routine work	
"	19	/7	Evacuated 7 animals to Base	
"	20	/7	Routine work	
"	21	/7	Evacuated 23 animals to Base	
"	22	/7	Routine work	
"	23	/7	Routine work	
"	24	/7	Evacuated 23 animals to Base	
"	25	/7	Evacuated 4 mules. Routine work. 4 men attached for duty from 94 I. Bde	

Army Form C. 2118

WAR DIARY
or
INTELLIGENCE SUMMARY 4/1st M.V.S.
(Erase heading not required.)

Instructions regarding War Diaries and Intelligence Summaries are contained in F. S. Regs., Part II. and the Staff Manual respectively. Title Pages will be prepared in manuscript.

Place	Date	Hour	Summary of Events and Information	Remarks and references to Appendices
Field	26/4/17		Routine work -	App
"	27/4/17		Routine work -	App
"	28/4/17		9 animals evacuated to Base	App
"	29/4/17		Routine work	App
"	30/4/17		Routine work	App

G.H.Kuecher
Capt AVC.
41st Mob. Vet. Sec.

WAR DIARY or INTELLIGENCE SUMMARY

41st M.V.S.

Place	Date	Hour	Summary of Events and Information	Remarks and references to Appendices
Field	1-12-17		Evacuated 29 animals to Base	GW
"	2-12-17		Routine work	GW
"	3-12-17		Routine work	GW
"	4-12-17		Routine work	GW
"	5-12-17		Evacuated 17 arrivals to Base – 4 lightly attacked returned to units	GW
"	6-12-17		Evacuated 24 arrivals to Base	GW
"	7-12-17		Routine work	GW
"	8-12-17		Evacuated 20 animals	GW
"	9-12-17		Routine work	GW
"	10-12-17		Routine work	GW
"	11-12-17		Evacuated 13 animals to Base	GW
"	12-12-17		Routine work	GW
"	13-12-17		Routine work	GW
"	14-12-17		Routine work	GW
"	15-12-17		Evacuated 21 animals to Base	GW

WAR DIARY
or
INTELLIGENCE SUMMARY

(Erase heading not required.)

41st M.V.S.

Army Form C. 2118

Place	Date	Hour	Summary of Events and Information	Remarks and references to Appendices
Field	16-12-17		Routine work	
"	17-12-17		Routine work	
"	18-12-17		Routine work	
"	19-12-17		Evacuated 12 animals to O.R.m.	
"	20-12-17		Routine work	
"	21-12-17		Evacuated 10 animals to O.R.m.	
"	22-12-17		Routine work	
"	23-12-17		Routine work	
"	24-12-17		Routine work	
"	25-12-17		Routine work	
"	26-12-17		Routine work	
"	27-12-17		Routine work	
"	28-12-17		Evacuated 27 animals to O.R.m.	
"	29-12-17		Routine work	
"	30-12-17		Routine work	
"	31-12-17		Routine work	

O.C. 41st M.V.S.

Army Form C. 2118

WAR DIARY
or
INTELLIGENCE SUMMARY 41st Mob: Vety: Sect.
(Erase heading not required.)

Vol 23

Place	Date	Hour	Summary of Events and Information	Remarks and references to Appendices
Field	1-1-18		Routine work	
"	2-1-18		Evacuated 17 animals to Base	
"	3-1-18		Routine work	
"	4-1-18		Evacuated 17 animals to Base	
"	5-1-18		Routine work	
"	6-1-18		Routine work. Assumed duties of DADVS during absence on leave of Maj. Matthews D.S.O.	
"	7-1-18		Routine work	
"	8-1-18		Routine work	
"	9-1-18		Evacuated 38 animals to Base	
"	10-1-18		Routine work	
"	11-1-18		Routine work	
"	12-1-18		Routine work	
"	13-1-18		Routine work	
"	14-1-18		Routine work	
"	15-1-18		Routine work	
"	16-1-18		Evacuated 22 animals to 14th Veterinary Hospital	
"	17-1-18		Routine work	

WAR DIARY
or
INTELLIGENCE SUMMARY 41st M.V.S.
(Erase heading not required.)

Army Form C. 2118

Place	Date	Hour	Summary of Events and Information	Remarks and references to Appendices
Field	18-1-18		Routine work	GHH
"	19-1-18		Evacuated 2 animals to Base	GHH
"	20-1-18		Routine work	GHH
"	21-1-18		Routine work	GHH
"	22-1-18		Routine work	GHH
"	23-1-18		Routine work	GHH
"	24-1-18		Evacuated 18 animals to Base - Assumed Vety charge of Division Capt Allen on leave	GHH
"	25-1-18		Routine work	GHH
"	26-1-18		Routine work	GHH
"	27-1-18		Routine work	GHH
"	28-1-18		Routine work	GHH
"	29-1-18		Routine work	GHH
"	30-1-18		Evacuated 16 animals to Base	GHH
"	31-1-18		Routine work	GHH

Arthur Captner
O.C. 41st Mob Vet Sec.

Army Form C. 2118

WAR DIARY
or
INTELLIGENCE SUMMARY

(Erase heading not required.)

41st M.V.S. 3/2

Vol 24

19__

Instructions regarding War Diaries and Intelligence Summaries are contained in F. S. Regs., Part II. and the Staff Manual respectively. Title Pages will be prepared in manuscript.

Place	Date	Hour	Summary of Events and Information	Remarks and references to Appendices
Field	1-2-19		Routine Work	pell
"	2-2-19		Routine Work	pell
"	3-2-19		Evacuated 5 animals to Base	pell
"	4-2-19		Routine work	pell
"	5-2-19		Inspected by D.D.V.S. 1st Army	pell
"	6-2-19		Routine Work	pell
"	7-2-19		Evacuated 21	pell
"	8-2-19		Routine Work	pell
"	9-2-19		Routine Work	pell
"	10-2-19		Routine Work	pell
"	11-2-19		Evacuated 14 animals to Base	pell
"	12-2-19		Routine Work	pell
"	13-2-19		Routine Work	pell
"	14-2-19		Routine Work	pell
"	15-2-19		Evacuated 8 animals to Base	pell
"	16-2-19		Routine Work	pell
"	17-2-19		Routine Work	pell

WAR DIARY
or
INTELLIGENCE SUMMARY. 41st M.V.S.

Army Form C. 2118.

Place	Date	Hour	Summary of Events and Information	Remarks and references to Appendices
Field	18-2-18		Routine work	
"	19-2-18		Routine work	
"	20-2-18		Routine work	
"	21-2-18		Evacuated 13 animals to Base	
"	22-2-18		Routine work	
"	23-2-18		Routine work	
"	24-2-18		Routine work	
"	25-2-18		Routine work	
"	26-2-18		Routine work	
"	27-2-18		Routine work	
"	28-2-18		Routine work	

O.C. 41st M.V.S. Vet. Ser.

WAR DIARY
or
INTELLIGENCE SUMMARY

Army Form C. 2118.

41st M.V.S.

Place	Date	Hour	Summary of Events and Information	Remarks and references to Appendices
Field	1-3-18		16 Animals evacuated to Base	
"	2-3-18		Routine work	
"	3-3-18		Hand over Section to Capt Bryant. Capt Bulletin proceeded on 14 days leave to the United Kingdom	
"	4-3-18		Moved to VANDELICOURT	
"	5-3-18		Routine work	
"	6-3-18		11 Animals evacuated B.Base	
"	7-3-18		Routine work	
"	8-3-18		Routine work	
"	9-3-18		Routine work	
"	10-3-18		Routine work	
"	11-3-18		Routine work	
"	12-3-18		Routine work	
"	13-3-18		8 Animals evacuated B.Base	
"	14-3-18		Routine work	
"	15-3-18		Routine work	

WAR DIARY or INTELLIGENCE SUMMARY

Army Form C. 2118.

41st M.V.S

Place	Date	Hour	Summary of Events and Information	Remarks and references to Appendices
"	16-3-18		Routine work	
"	17-3-18		Routine work to prepare to proceed	
"	18-3-18		Ord horse went to prepare to proceed, First Army	
"	19-3-18		Capt BUTCHER returned from leave & assumed command of unit from Capt BRIGHT	
"	20-3-18		Routine work	
"	21-3-18		Routine work	
"	22-3-18		Evacuated 17 animals to Base - Marched to BASSEUX	
"	23-3-18		Routine work	
"	24-3-18		Marched to DOUCHY-Les-AYETTE	
"	25-3-18		Marched to HUMBERCAMPS	
"	26-3-18		Ordered to march to WARLUS - reached BERNEVILLE & ordered to return to HUMBERCAMPS again	
"	27-3-18		Evacuated 16 animals to Base	
"	28-3-18		Routine work	
"	29-3-18		Evacuated 16 animals to Base	
"	30-3-18		Evacuated 15 animals to Base	
"	31-3-18		Routine work	

Note:
Transport not working well owing to float which delays movement of section. Transport available 1 A.S. limber wagon & 1 trough float. This float was sent in exchange of 1 G.S. limber - it is absolutely useless. Transport used in the march over roads rendered bad by weather & heavy traffic. The carrying of the body of the float is not sufficient for in an attempt bringing in the dead surface. It is a constant danger as it is liable at any movement to become either up side down or to a standstill. It cannot carry an ordinary load as it is a cumbersome & heavy vehicle. It is unfit for what is a built up station, to carry sick horses but as a transport wagon for wounded.

[signatures]
Capt.
O.C. 41st M.V.S.

B.E.F. FRANCE
Date of forming this expeditionary force, 9th March 1916.

Ambulance Horse
Horse-Float.

Army Form C. 2118.

WAR DIARY
or
INTELLIGENCE SUMMARY.
(Erase heading not required.)

41st M.V.S.

Place	Date	Hour	Summary of Events and Information	Remarks and references to Appendices
Field	1-4-18		Marched from HUMBER CAMP at 7.30 a.m. to LUCHEUX, arrived in field	
"	2-4-18		Marched at 7.30 a.m. for CAMBLIGNEUL about 25 K. arrived 2.30 p.m. Horses picketed in open field - men in billets	
"	3-4-18		Routine work -	
"	4-4-18		Routine work - 4th group from Hdqrs Div S entrance moving away Sec	
"	5-4-18		Routine work	
"	6-4-18		Routine work - received 9 horses for evacuation from 1 London M.V.S who were moving away	
"	7-4-18		Routine work	
"	8-4-18		Routine work	
"	9-4-18		Routine work	
"	10-4-18		Marched at 8 p.m. for BOURECQ (LILLERS) arrived 3 a.m. (bivouac) Handed over 11 horses to Canadian M.V.S at APREZ	
"	11-4-18		Marched at 9 a.m. for BORRÉ via S. VENANT & HAZEBROUCK arrived at 6 p.m. Bivouacked in Place old l'Eglise	
"	12-4-18		Routine work	
"	13-4-18		Marched at 1 a.m. for LES CASEAUX via HAZEBROUCK arrived at 5 A.M. bivouaced in field	
"	14-4-18		Evacuated by road 17 minutes to 23 Vet. Hosp. at S. OMER	
"	15-4-18		Routine work	

Army Form C. 2118.

WAR DIARY
or
INTELLIGENCE SUMMARY. 41st M.V.S.
(Erase heading not required.)

Instructions regarding War Diaries and Intelligence Summaries are contained in F.S. Regs., Part II. and the Staff Manual respectively. Title pages will be prepared in manuscript.

Place	Date	Hour	Summary of Events and Information	Remarks and references to Appendices
Field	16-4-18		Routine work	App
"	17-4-18		Evacuated 19 animals to S. OMER (23rd Vety. Hosp) by road	App
"	18-4-18		Routine work	App
"	19-4-18		Evacuated 16 animals to XV Corps Evacuating Station at LYNDE, Station arrived at 1.30 pm to Chateau near EBBLINGHEM & bivouaced	App
"	20-4-18		Marched from last camp to camp on S. OMER - HAZEBROUCK road about 2 kilometres from WALLON CAPPEL. (Map 27 - W20.b.9.4)	App
"	21-4-18		Routine work	App
"	22-4-18		Evacuated 7 animals to XV Corps Evacuating Station	App
"	23-4-18		Routine work	App
"	24-4-18		Evacuated 18 animals to XV Corps Evacuating Station	App
"	25-4-18		Routine work 15	App
"	26-4-18		Evacuated 11 animals to XV Corps Evacuating Station	App
"	27-4-18		Routine work	App
"	28-4-18		Evacuated 7 animals to XV Corps Evac. Station - Marched at 3.30 am & HONDEGHEM arrived 11 a.m.	App
"	29-4-18		Routine work	App
"	30-4-18		Routine work	App

Date of formation of 41st M.V.S. — 4th Oct /15.
Date of proceeding overseas from U.K. — 15 Jan /16.

G.W. Baird Cpt.
Capt. A.V.C.
O.C. 41st M.V.S.

Confidential

War Diary.
41st Mob. Vet. Section.

May, 1918.

Volume XXIX
No 27

Army Form C. 2118.

WAR DIARY
or
INTELLIGENCE SUMMARY. 41st M.V.S.
(Erase heading not required.)

Place	Date	Hour	Summary of Events and Information	Remarks and references to Appendices
Field	1-5-18		8 animals evacuated to XV Corps E.S. (No 15)	Ypres
"	2-5-18		9 animals evacuated to XV Corps E.S. (No 15)	Ypres
"	3-5-18		9 animals evacuated to No 15. E.S.	Ypres
"	4-5-18		Routine work	Ypres
"	5-5-18		Routine work	Ypres
"	6-5-18		Routine work	Ypres
"	7-5-18		8 animals evacuated to No 15- E.S.	Ypres
"	8-5-18		Routine work	Ypres
"	9-5-18		14 animals evacuated to No 15. E.S.	Ypres
"	10-5-18		Routine work	Ypres
"	11-5-18		8 animals evacuated to No. 15. E.S.	Ypres
"	12-5-18		Routine work	Ypres
"	13-5-18		18 animals evacuated to No 15. E.S.	Ypres
"	14-5-18		Routine work	Ypres
"	15-5-18		13 animals evacuated to No 15 E.S.	Ypres
"	16-5-18		Routine work	Ypres

Army Form C. 2118.

WAR DIARY
or
INTELLIGENCE SUMMARY. 4/14 M.V.S.
(Erase heading not required.)

Instructions regarding War Diaries and Intelligence Summaries are contained in F.S. Regs., Part II. and the Staff Manual respectively. Title pages will be prepared in manuscript.

Place	Date	Hour	Summary of Events and Information	Remarks and references to Appendices
Field	17-5-18		Evacuated 5 animals to No. 15. E.9.	
"	18-5-18		Evacuated 11 animals to No. 15. E.S.	
"	19-5-18		Routine work	
"	20-5-18		Evacuated 8 animals to No. 15. E.9.	
"	21-5-18		Evacuated 15 animals to No. 15. E.9.	
"	22-5-18		Evacuated 1 animal to No. 15. E.S.	
"	23-5-18		Evacuated 10 animals to No. 15. E.9.	
"	24-5-18		Marched from HONDEGHEM at 9.30 a.m. to LA BELLE CROIX arrived at 12 noon.	
"	25-5-18		Routine work	
"	26-5-18		1 animal evacuated to No. 23 V. Hospital at S. OMER	
"	27-5-18		Routine work	
"	28-5-18		Evacuated 3 animals to No. 23 V. Hospital S. OMER	
"	29-5-18		Evacuated 14 animals to No. 23 V. Hosp.	
"	30-5-18		Marched from LA BELLE CROIX to BAYENGHEM at 9.30 a.m.	
"	31-5-18		Evacuated 11 animals to No. 23 V. Hospital	

1st June/18

J.W. Buckler Captain.
O.C. 4/14 M.V.S.

Army Form C. 2118.

WAR DIARY
or
INTELLIGENCE SUMMARY.
(Erase heading not required.)

4/1st M.V.S.

Place	Date	Hour	Summary of Events and Information	Remarks and references to Appendices
Field	1-6-18		Routine Work	
"	2-6-18		1 horse evacuated to No 23 V.Hosp. at S.OMER	
"	3-6-18		9 horses evacuated to No 23 V.H.	
"	4-6-18		Routine Work	
"	5-6-18		Routine Work	
"	6-6-18		Routine Work	
"	7-6-18		12 Animals evacuated to No 23 V.H.	
"	8-6-18		Routine Work	
"	9-6-18		Routine Work	
"	10-6-18		1 animal evacuated to No 23 V.H. Capt Paulton proceeded to LUMBRES to relieve criminals all horses from EGYPT belonging to 94th Inf. Bde. Major Matthew took over A.V.C. command of Section	
"	11-6-18		11 animals evacuated to No 23 V.H.	
"	12-6-18		Routine Work. Capt Paulton returned to Sect. having completed his duties at LUMBRES & resumed command of the Sect.	
"	13-6-18		Routine Work	

Army Form C. 2118.

WAR DIARY
or
INTELLIGENCE SUMMARY.
(Erase heading not required.)

Instructions regarding War Diaries and Intelligence Summaries are contained in F. S. Regs., Part II. and the Staff Manual respectively. Title pages will be prepared in manuscript.

Place	Date	Hour	Summary of Events and Information	Remarks and references to Appendices
Field	14-6-18		Evacuated 7 animals to 23 V. Hosp. B. OMER	
"	15-6-18		Routine work	
"	16-6-18		Routine work	
"	17-6-18		Routine work	
"	18-6-18		Routine work	
"	19-6-18		Evacuated 5 animals to No. 23 Vet. Hosp. B. OMER	
"	20-6-18		Routine work	
"	21-6-18		Routine work	
"	22-6-18		Marched from BANDRINGHAM to S. LEGER. Evacuated 5 animals to No. 23 V. Hosp. B. OMER	
"	23-6-18		Evacuated 2 animals by motor ambulance to No. 23 Hosp. B. OMER	
"	24-6-18		Evacuated 6 animals to No. 15 V.E.S.	
"	25-6-18		Routine work	
"	26-6-18		Evacuated 6 animals to No. 15 V.E.S.	
"	27-6-18		Evacuated 2 animals to No. 15 V.E.S.	
"	28-6-18		Evacuated 3 animals to No. 15 V.E.S.	
"	29-6-18		Evacuated 5 animals to No. 15 V.E.S.	
"	30-6-18		Evacuated 1 animal to No. 15 E.V.S.	

Tapp Capt.
O.C. H.1 & M.V.S.

Army Form C. 2118.

WAR DIARY
or
INTELLIGENCE SUMMARY.   41st M.V.S.

(Erase heading not required.)

Place	Date	Hour	Summary of Events and Information	Remarks and references to Appendices
Field	1-7-18		Routine work	
"	2-7-18		Evacuated 8 animals to N°15 V.E.S.	
"	3-7-18		Evacuated 4 animals to N°15 V.E.S.	
"	4-7-18		Routine work	
"	5-7-18		Evacuated 6 animals to N°15 V.E.S.	
"	6-7-18		Routine work	
"	7-7-18		Routine work	
"	8-7-18		Evacuated 2 animals to N°15 V.E.S.	
"	9-7-18		Evacuated 4 animals to N°15 V.E.S.	
"	10-7-18		Routine work	
"	11-7-18		Evacuated 11 animals to N°15 V.E.S.	
"	12-7-18		Evacuated 41 animals to N°15 V.E.S.	
"	13-7-18		Routine work	
"	14-7-18		Routine work	
"	15-7-18		Evacuated 5 animals to N°15 V.E.S.	
"	16-7-18		Evacuated 4 animals to N°15 V.E.S.	
"	17-7-18		Routine work	

Army Form C. 2118.

WAR DIARY
or
INTELLIGENCE SUMMARY.   41st M.V.S.

(Erase heading not required.)

Instructions regarding War Diaries and Intelligence Summaries are contained in F. S. Regs., Part II. and the Staff Manual respectively. Title pages will be prepared in manuscript.

Place	Date	Hour	Summary of Events and Information	Remarks and references to Appendices
Field	18-7-18		Evacuated 6 animals to No 15 V.E.S. D.D.V.S. 2nd Army inspected Section	
"	19-7-18		Routine work - Accompanied duties of D.A.D.V.S. during absence on leave of Maj. Matthews	
"	20-7-18		Evacuated 7 animals to No 15 V.E.S.	
"	21-7-18		Routine work	
"	22-7-18		Evacuated 9 animals to No 15 V.E.S.	
"	23-7-18		Evacuated 3 animals to No 15 V.E.S.	
"	24-7-18		Routine work	
"	25-7-18		Routine work	
"	26-7-18		Routine work	
"	27-7-18		Routine work	
"	28-7-18		Evacuated 3 animals to No 15 V.E.S.	
"	29-7-18		Evacuated 3 animals to No 15 V.E.S.	
"	30-7-18		Evacuated 4 animals to No 15 V.E.S.	
"	31-7-18		Evacuated 3 animals to No 15 V.E.S.	

W. Whitelaw
O.C. 41st M.V.S.

Army Form C. 2118.

WAR DIARY
or
INTELLIGENCE SUMMARY.

(Erase heading not required.)

41st M.V.S.

Vol 30

Place	Date	Hour	Summary of Events and Information	Remarks and references to Appendices
In the Field	1-8-18		Routine work	
"	2-8-18		Routine work	
"	3-8-18		Routine work - Maj. Mathews returned from leave & resumed duties of D.A.D.V.S. for Capt Butcher	
"	4-8-18		3 animals evacuated to No 15 V.E.S.	
"	5-8-18		3 animals evacuated to No 15 V.E.S.	
"	6-8-18		4 animals evacuated to No 15 V.E.S.	
"	7-8-18		3 animals evacuated to No 15 V.E.S.	
"	8-8-18		2 animals evacuated to No 15 V.E.S.	
"	9-8-18		Routine work	
"	10-8-18		3 animals evacuated to No 15 V.E.S.	
"	11-8-18		Routine work	
"	12-8-18		3 animals evacuated to No 15 V.E.S.	
"	13-8-18		Routine work	
"	14-8-18		6 animals evacuated to No 15 V.E.S.	
"	15-8-18		Routine work	
"	16-8-18		Routine work	
"	17-8-18		1 animal evacuated to No 16 V.E.S.	

Army Form C. 2118.

WAR DIARY
or
INTELLIGENCE SUMMARY.

(Erase heading not required.)

41st M.V.S.

Instructions regarding War Diaries and Intelligence Summaries are contained in F. S. Regs., Part II. and the Staff Manual respectively. Title pages will be prepared in manuscript.

Place	Date	Hour	Summary of Events and Information	Remarks and references to Appendices
In the Field	18-8-18		Routine work	S/W
"	19-8-18		2 animals evacuated to No 15 V.E.S.	L/W
"	20-8-18		do	L/W
"	21-8-18		Routine work	L/W
"	22-8-18		do	L/W
"	23-8-18		do	L/W
"	24-8-18		4 Animals evacuated to No 15 V.E.S. Moved to V.C.C.S. 6 Sheet 27.	L/W
"	25-8-18		Routine work	L/W
"	26-8-18		do	L/W
"	27-8-18		3 Animals evacuated to No 15 V.E.S	L/W
"	28-8-18		Routine work	L/W
"	29-8-18		5 Animals evacuated to No 15 V.E.S	L/W
"	30-8-18		2 do	L/W
"	31-8-18		Moved section to V.C.C.S. 2. Sheet 27	L/W

W.Bright Capt. A.V.C
O.C. 41st M.V.S.

Army Form C. 2118.

WAR DIARY
or
INTELLIGENCE SUMMARY.

41st Mobile Veterinary Section

(Erase heading not required.)

Vol 3 &

Place	Date	Hour	Summary of Events and Information	Remarks and references to Appendices
Field	1. 9/15	—	Routine work	S.193
"	2. 9/15	—	3 Animals evacuated to 15" V.E.S.	2/40 S193
"	3. 9/15	—	Routine work	S193
"	4. 9/15	—	3 Animals evacuated to 15" V.E.S.	S193
"	5. 9/15	—	6 Animals evacuated to 75" V.E.S. Capt Butcher returned command of the Section from Capt Bright A.V.C.	G.H.H
"	6. 9/15	—	Marched to CAESTRE. 2 Animals evacuated by motor amb. to No 2 D Vet. Hosp.	G.H.H
"	7. 9/15	—	3 animals evacuated to 15" V.E.S.	G.H.H
"	8. 9/15	—	2 animals evacuated to 75" V.E.S. Marched to X 14 c 27 c 20 sheet 27	G.H.H
"	9. 9/15	—	5 Animals evacuated to 75" V.E.S.	G.H.H
"	10. 9/15	—	Routine Work	G.H.H
"	11. 9/15	—	11 Evacuated to No 15 V.E.S.	G.H.H
"	12. 9/15	—	11 Evacuated to No 15 V.E.S.	G.H.H
"	13. 9/15	—	Routine work	G.H.H
"	14. 9/15	—	8 Evacuated to No 15 V.E.S.	G.H.H
"	15. 9/15	—	Routine work	G.H.H

Army Form C. 2118.

WAR DIARY
or
INTELLIGENCE SUMMARY.

(Erase heading not required.)

41st Mobile Veterinary Section

Instructions regarding War Diaries and Intelligence Summaries are contained in F. S. Regs., Part II. and the Staff Manual respectively. Title pages will be prepared in manuscript.

Place	Date	Hour	Summary of Events and Information	Remarks and references to Appendices
Field	16-9-18		7 Evacuated to No. 15 V.E.S.	
"	17-9-18		3 Evacuated to No. 15 V.E.S.	
"	18-9-18		Routine work	
"	19-9-18		4 animals evacuated to No. 15 V.E.S.	
"	20-9-18		Routine work	
"	21-9-18		4 animals evacuated to No. 15 V.E.S.	
"	22-9-18		10 animals evacuated to No. 15 V.E.S.	
"	23-9-18		2 animals evacuated to No. 15 V.E.S.	
"	24-9-18		Routine work	
"	25-9-18		4 animals evacuated to No. 15 V.E.S.	
"	26-9-18		2 " " "	
"	27-9-18		Routine work	
"	28-9-18		1 animal evacuated to No. 15 V.E.S.	
"	29-9-18		5 " "	
"	30-9-18		2 " "	

GH Reed Capt
O.C. 41 M.V.S.

WAR DIARY
or
INTELLIGENCE SUMMARY

41st Mobile Veterinary Section.

Army Form C. 2118.

Vol 53

Place	Date	Hour	Summary of Events and Information	Remarks and references to Appendices
Field	1-10-18		Routine work	
"	2-10-18		66 Animals evacuated to No 15 V.E.S.	
"	3-10-18		Routine work	
"	4-10-18		Routine Work	
"	5-10-18		3 Animals evacuated to No 15 V.E.S. & 2 to No 23 Vety Hosp. 8 UMER by flat	
"	6-10-18		2 Animals evacuated to No 15 V.E.S.	
"	7-10-18		2 Animals evacuated to No 15 V.E.S. Sect marched to DE SEULE (35/B.1a 57)	
"	8-10-18		Routine work	
"	9-10-18		Routine work	
"	10-10-18		Routine work	
"	11-10-18		Routine work	
"	12-10-18		Routine work	
"	13-10-18		1 Animal evacuated to No 15 V.E.S.	
"	14-10-18		Routine work	
"	15-10-18		Routine work. 3 Animals evacuated to No 15 V.E.S.	
"	16-10-18		Animals evacuated to No 15 V.E.S.	
"	17		Routine work	

Army Form C. 2118.

WAR DIARY
or
INTELLIGENCE SUMMARY.

(Erase heading not required.)

41st Mobile Veterinary Section

Instructions regarding War Diaries and Intelligence Summaries are contained in F.S. Regs., Part II. and the Staff Manual respectively. Title pages will be prepared in manuscript.

Place	Date	Hour	Summary of Events and Information	Remarks and references to Appendices
Field	18-10-18		4 Evacuated to No 15 V.E.S.	JW
Field	19-10-18		3 animals evacuated to No 15 V.E.S. Section marched to LA BASSE VILLE	JW JW
"	20-10-18		Marched at 9.30 for QUESNOY arrived 12 noon. Received orders at 5 pm to march to LE JAMBON, arrived there at 8 p.m.	JW JW
"	21-10-18		Marched to ROUBAIX	JW
"	22-10-18		Routine work. Section in wool factory Rue ROUBAIX	JW JW
"	23-10-18		Routine work	JW
"	24-10-18		13 animals evacuated to No 15 V.E.S.	JW
"	25-10-18		Routine work	JW
"	26-10-18		Routine work	JW
"	27-10-18		7 animals handed over to 37st M.V.S. Section marched to WERNE	JW
"	28-10-18		Routine work	JW
"	29-10-18		Routine work	JW
"	30-10-18		3 animals evacuated to No 2 V.E.S.	JW
"	31-10-18		Routine work	JW

W.J.Kircher Capt
O.C. 41st M.V.S.

Army Form C. 2118.

WAR DIARY
or
INTELLIGENCE SUMMARY.
(Erase heading not required.)

41st - Mob. Vet. Sec.

Place	Date	Hour	Summary of Events and Information	Remarks and references to Appendices
Field	1-11-18		3 animals evacuated to No 2 V.E.S	
"	2-11-18		Routine work	
"	3-11-18		6 animals evacuated to No 2 V.E.S. Section marched from CUERNE to BLANC FOUR (sheet 20 x 19 d. 1.3.)	
"	4-11-18		Routine work	
"	5-11-18		Routine work	
"	6-11-18		Evacuated 12 animals to No 15 V.E.S.	
"	7-11-18		Evacuated 6 animals to No 15 V.E.S.	
"	8-11-18		Marched from BLANC FOUR to near COURTRAI (sheet 29. H 3 & 4.8)	
"	9-11-18		Marched from COURTRAI to near SWEVEGHEM (sheet 29. N 5 d 2.5")	
"	10-11-18		Evacuated 1 animal to No 10 V.E.S. Routine work - 7 animals evacuated to No 7 V.E.S.	
"	11-11-18		Rode to RUYEN (sheet 29 V.b.5) to try to get in touch with D.A.D.V.S. 74 Div. but failed to do so	
"	12-11-18		Completely out of touch of Division + D.A.D.V.S. Also have no knowledge of location of V.E.S. No Communication (orders etc) received for certain duties evacuated from BLANC FOUR on the 8th (continued)	

Army Form C. 2118.

WAR DIARY
of
INTELLIGENCE SUMMARY.

(Erase heading not required.)

41st M.V.S.

Instructions regarding War Diaries and Intelligence Summaries are contained in F. S. Regs., Part II. and the Staff Manual respectively. Title pages will be prepared in manuscript.

Place	Date	Hour	Summary of Events and Information	Remarks and references to Appendices
Field	12-11-18		Met MaA & QMG who passing through SWEVEGHEM & he gave us orders to march to AVELGHEM. Section marched at 2.15 pm & arrived at AVELGHEM at 5 pm.	
"	13-11-18		Routine work	
"	14-11-18		Routine work	
"	15-11-18		Marched from AVELGHEM at 10 am, & arrived at POTTELBERG (Map 29.M.12.Z.4.8)	
"	16-11-18		Routine work	
"	17-11-18		Routine work	
"	18-11-18		Routine work	
"	19-11-18		Routine work	
"	20-11-18		4 animals evacuated to No 7 V.E.S.	
"	21-11-18		Routine work	
"	22-11-18		6 animals evacuated to No 7 V.E.S.	
"	23-11-18		Routine work	
"	24-11-18		8 animals evacuated to No 7 V.E.S.	
"	25-11-18		7 anim. also wounded to No 7 V.E.S. Marched to MENIN.	

Army Form C. 2118.

WAR DIARY
~~INTELLIGENCE SUMMARY.~~

(Erase heading not required.)

41st M.T.S.

Instructions regarding War Diaries and Intelligence Summaries are contained in F. S. Regs., Part II. and the Staff Manual respectively. Title pages will be prepared in manuscript.

Place	Date	Hour	Summary of Events and Information	Remarks and references to Appendices
Field	26-11-18		Marched to YPRES	
"	27-11-18		Marched to ABEELE	
"	28-11-18		Marched to STAPLE	
"	29-11-18		Marched to WIZERNES	
"	30-11-18		Marched to LEAUWETTE	

20/11/18.

Capt
O.C. 41st M.T.S.

9/2

31

Army Form C. 2118.

WAR DIARY
or
INTELLIGENCE SUMMARY.   41st Mobile Veterinary Section
(Erase heading not required.)

Instructions regarding War Diaries and Intelligence Summaries are contained in F. S. Regs., Part II and the Staff Manual respectively. Title pages will be prepared in manuscript.

D.A.D.V.S.
31st DIVISION
No. S/458
Date 9/1/19

WO 95 35

Place	Date	Hour	Summary of Events and Information	Remarks and references to Appendices
Field	1-12-18		Marched from IZEAUWETTE to AUDENTHUN	GWB
"	2-12-18		Routine work	GWB
"	3-12-18		Routine work	GWB
"	4-12-18		4 animals evacuated to No. 23 V. Hosp.	GWB
"	5-12-18		Marched from AUDENTHUN to BLENDECQUE	GWB
"	6-12-18		Routine work	GWB
"	7-12-18		Capt BUTCHER ordered to No 3 Canadian Hosp. Sick	GWB
Field	8.12.18		Major MATTHEW RAVC took charge during Capt Butcher's absence	RCM
"	9.12.18		Routine work	RCM
"	10.12.18		Routine work	RCM
"	11.12.18		Routine work	RCM
"	12.12.18		Routine work	RCM
"	13.12.18		Routine work	RCM
"	14.12.18		Routine work	RCM
"	15.12.18		Routine work	RCM
"	16.12.18		Routine work	RCM

Army Form C. 2118.

WAR DIARY
or
INTELLIGENCE SUMMARY.
(Erase heading not required.)

4 st Mobile Vety Section

D.A.D.V.S.
31st DIVISION

Place	Date	Hour	Summary of Events and Information	Remarks and references to Appendices
Field	17/12/15	—	Capt S.P. Bright M.R.C.V.S. took Veterinary Charge. 77 Animals evacuated to 23rd Vet. Hospital	AV&B
"	18/12/15	—	Routine	AV&B
"	19/12/15	—	46 Animals evacuated to 23rd Veterinary Hospital	AV&B
"	20/12/15	—	Routine	AV&B
"	21/12/15	—	Routine	AV&B
"	22/12/15	—	10 Animals evacuated to 23rd Vet. Hospital	AV&B
"	23/12/15	—	4 Animals evacuated to 23rd Vet. Hospital	AV&B
"	24/12/15	—	Routine	AV&B
"	25/12/15	—	Routine	AV&B
"	26/12/15	—	Routine	AV&B
"	27/12/15	—	Routine	AV&B
"	28/12/15	—	Routine	AV&B
"	29/12/15	—	Routine	AV&B
"	30/12/15	—	1 Animal evacuated to 23rd Vet. Hospital	AV&B
"	31/12/15	—	2 Animals do	AV&B

WAR DIARY or INTELLIGENCE SUMMARY.

Army Form C. 2118.

41st M.V.S.

(Erase heading not required.)

Place	Date	Hour	Summary of Events and Information	Remarks and references to Appendices
Field	1/7/19	—	Routine	
"	2/7	—	Routine	
"	3/7/19	—	3 Animals evacuated to 23rd Vet: Hospital. This includes 2 stray animals from missing 31st Divn.	
"	4/7/19		Capt. G.M. BUTCHER resumed command of Sect: on discharge from hosp: const.	
"	5/7/19		3 animals evacuated to 23 V. Hosp.	
"	6/7/19		4 animals evacuated to 23 V. Hosp.	
"	7/7/19		4 animals evacuated to 23 V. Hosp.	
"	8/7/19		8 animals evacuated to 23 V. Hosp.	
"	9/7/19		10 animals evacuated to 23 V. Hosp. (including 9 Brood mares)	
"	10/7/19		Routine	
"	11/7/19		Routine	
"	12/7/19		Routine	
"	13/7/19		4 animals evacuated to 23 V. Hosp.	
"	14/7/19		Routine	
"	15/7/19		Routine	
"	16/7/19		2 animals evacuated to No. 23 V. Hosp.	

Army Form C. 2118.

WAR DIARY
or
INTELLIGENCE SUMMARY.

(Erase heading not required.)

41st M.V.S.

D.A.D.V.S.
31st DIVISION.

Instructions regarding War Diaries and Intelligence Summaries are contained in F. S. Regs., Part II. and the Staff Manual respectively. Title pages will be prepared in manuscript.

Place	Date	Hour	Summary of Events and Information	Remarks and references to Appendices
Field	17/7/19		4 animals evacuated to 23 V. Hosp.	
"	18/7/19		1 animal evacuated to 23 V. Hosp	
"	19/7/19		3 animals evacuated to 23 V. Hosp.	
"	20/7/19		Routine work	
"	21/7/19		4 animals evacuated to No. 23 Vet. Hosp.	
"	22/7/19		Routine work	
"	23/7/19		2 animals evacuated to No. 23 V. Hosp.	
"	24/7/19		Routine work	
"	25/7/19		2 animals evacuated to No. 23 V. Hosp.	
"	26/7/19		Routine work	
"	27/7/19		10 animals evacuated to No. 23 V. Hosp.	
"	28/7/19		Routine	
"	29/7/19		5 animals evacuated to No. 23 V. Hosp.	
"	30/7/19		3 animals evacuated to No. 23 V. Hosp.	
"	31/7/19		Routine work	

G.M.Butcher Capt.
O.C. 41st MOB. VET. SECT.

WAR DIARY
or
INTELLIGENCE SUMMARY.
(Erase heading not required.)

Army Form C. 2118.

41st M.V.S.

Place	Date	Hour	Summary of Events and Information	Remarks and references to Appendices
Field	1-2-19		5 animals evacuated to 23rd Vet. Hosp.	
"	2-2-19		2 animals evacuated to 23rd Vet. Hosp.	
"	3-2-19		Routine work	
"	4-2-19		1 animal evacuated to 23rd Vet. Hosp.	
"	5-2-19		6 animals evacuated to 23rd Vet. Hosp.	
"	6-2-19		1 animal evacuated to 23rd Vet. Hosp.	
"	7-2-19		Routine work	
"	8-2-19		1 animals evacuated to 23 Vet. Hosp. S. OMER	
"	9-2-19		2 animals evacuated to 23rd Vet. Hosp.	
"	10-2-19		10 animals evacuated to 23rd Vet. Hosp.	
"	11-2-19		Routine work	
"	12-2-19		3 animals evacuated to 23rd Vet. Hosp.	
"	13-2-19		3 animals evacuated to 23rd Vet. Hosp.	
"	14-2-19		1 animals evacuated to No 23rd Vet. Hosp.	
"	15-2-19		Routine work	
"	16-2-19		Routine work	

Army Form C. 2118.

WAR DIARY
or
INTELLIGENCE SUMMARY. 41st M.V.S

(Erase heading not required.)

Instructions regarding War Diaries and Intelligence Summaries are contained in F. S. Regs., Part II. and the Staff Manual respectively. Title pages will be prepared in manuscript.

Place	Date	Hour	Summary of Events and Information	Remarks and references to Appendices
Field	17-2-19		2 animals evacuated to N.23 Vety. Hosp.	
"	18-2-19		4 animals evacuated to N.23 Vet. Hosp.	
"	19-2-19		1 animal evacuated to N.23 Vet. Hosp.	
"	20-2-19		Capt. Wright took Infirmary charge during Capt. Ruthries absence on leave to home evacuation	
"	21-2-19		Routine work	
"	22-2-19		3 animals evacuated to No. 2 & 3 Vety Hospital	
"	23-2-19		2 animals evacuated to No. 3 Vety Hospital	
"	24-2-19		Routine work	
"	25-2-19		Routine work	
"	26-2-19		4 animals evacuated to 2 & 3rd Vety Hospital	
"	27-2-19		do	
"	28-2-19		3 animals evacuated to 2 3rd Vety Hospital	

O.C. 41st

Army Form C. 2118.

WAR DIARY
or
INTELLIGENCE SUMMARY.
(Erase heading not required.)

Instructions regarding War Diaries and Intelligence Summaries are contained in F. S. Regs., Part II. and the Staff Manual respectively. Title pages will be prepared in manuscript.

Place	Date	Hour	Summary of Events and Information	Remarks and references to Appendices
Dundsgnea	1-3-19		7 Animals evacuated to 2.3 Vety Hospital	
"	2-3-19		2 Animals evacuated to No 2.3 Vety Hospital	
"	3-3-19		Routine work	
"	4-3-19		3 Animals evacuated to No 2.3 Vety Hospital	
"	5-3-19		1 Animal do	
"	6-3-19		2 Animals evacuated to 2.3rd Vety Hospital	
"	7-3-19		3 do	
"	8-3-19		3 do	
"	9-3-19		Routine work	
"	10-3-19		4 Animals evacuated to 2.3rd Vety Hospital	
"	11-3-19		Routine work	
"	12-3-19		4 Animals evacuated to 2.3rd Vety Hospital 3 Animals handed to Mob V.F.S. And 1 Sergeant transfd to 44th M.V.B.	
"	13-3-19		Routine work	
"	14-3-19		do	
"	15-3-19		do	

Army Form C. 2118.

WAR DIARY
or
INTELLIGENCE SUMMARY.
(Erase heading not required.)

Instructions regarding War Diaries and Intelligence Summaries are contained in F. S. Regs., Part II. and the Staff Manual respectively. Title pages will be prepared in manuscript.

Place	Date	Hour	Summary of Events and Information	Remarks and references to Appendices
Alexandria	16-3-19		1 animal evacuated to 23rd Vety Hospital	
"	17-3-19		Routine work	
"	18-3-19		do	
"	19-3-19		do	
"	20-3-19		do	
"	21-3-19		do	
"	22-3-19		do	
"	23-3-19		2 animals evacuated to 25th Vety Hospital	
"	24-3-19		Routine work	
"	25-3-19		2 animals evacuated to 23rd Vety Hospital	
"	26-3-19		Inspection of stain by Ordnance Staff	
"	27-3-19		1 animal evacuated to 23rd Vety Hospital	
"	28-3-19		Routine work	
"	29-3-19		do	
"	30-3-19		do	
"	31-3-19		do	

J.B.Bright
O.C. 41st M.V.S.

31

Army Form C. 2118.

WAR DIARY
or
INTELLIGENCE SUMMARY.
(Erase heading not required.)

4/1st Middlesex Yeomanry ?????

Instructions regarding War Diaries and Intelligence Summaries are contained in F.S. Regs., Part II. and the Staff Manual respectively. Title pages will be prepared in manuscript.

Place	Date	Hour	Summary of Events and Information	Remarks and references to Appendices
BLENDECQUES	1.4.19		Major R. Matthews took over	RCM
"	2.4.19		Routine work	RCM
"	3.4.19		Routine work	RCM
"	4.4.19		Routine work	RCM
"	5.4.19		Routine work	RCM
"	6.4.19		Routine work	RCM
"	7.4.19		Routine work	RCM
"	8.4.19	6	Capt. C.L. Taylor took over duties as O.C. H? Middx Yeo Sec	CLT
"	9.4.19		Routine work	CLT
"	10.4.19		Routine work	CLT
"	11.4.19		Routine work	CLT
"	12.4.19		Routine work	CLT
"	13.4.19		Routine work	CLT
"	14.4.19		Routine work	CLT
"	15.4.19		Routine work	CLT
"	16.4.19		Routine work	CLT

Army Form C. 2118.

WAR DIARY
or
INTELLIGENCE SUMMARY.
(Erase heading not required.)

41st Mobile Vety Section

Place	Date	Hour	Summary of Events and Information	Remarks and references to Appendices
Blendecques	17/4/19		Routine WnR	
"	18 4.19		Routine WnR	
"	19 4.19		Routine WnR	
"	20 4.19		Routine WnR	
"	21 4.19		Routine WnR. Reton. number change to 36 Mobile 21/4/19	
"	22-4-19		Routine Work	
"	23-4-19		Moved from Blendecques to Longuenesse	
Longuenesse	24-4-19		Attached to No 4 Coy 31st Divl Train	
"	25-4-19		Inspection of Stores by O.C. No 4 Coy. 31st D.T.	
"	26-4-19		Routine Work	
"	27-4-19		Routine Work	
"	28-4-19		Routine Work	
"	29-4-19		Routine Work	
"	30-4-19		Routine Work	

Phippss Capt
O.C. 41st Mob Vety Sect.

www.ingramcontent.com/pod-product-compliance
Lightning Source LLC
Chambersburg PA
CBHW081434160426
43193CB00013B/2275